Laughter Through Tears

J.M.G Lailvaux

"SOME TRUE LIFE STORIES ARE MEANT TO BE TOLD, READ AND PASSED ON."

"LAUGHTER THROUGH TEARS, IS ONE OF THOSE STORIES."

Dear Lauren,

Thank you so much for editing this book for me.

Gilbert.

December 2017.

FOREWORD

Ryan Lailvaux

It is a warm September morning. My Dad sits on my bed as he listens to a speech that I needed to practice.

"It's good," he declares. "Can I show you how I would deliver it?"

He takes my place near the door, with my prepared notes, and he recites the lines.

It is as though he is channelling Winston Churchill's spirit as he articulates the words with authority.

Wearily, he retakes his seat on the bed. He does not have the same energy as he used to. Inspired by his delivery, I jot down some notes. Even after thirty years, he still surprises me.

It had been a year since my Dad lay in the same bed, but in drastically different circumstances. I remember clearly where I was when I received that phone call, as many do when they get traumatic news. It was a Friday evening, and I had just walked in my apartment when the phone rang. It was my Dad. We spoke for a while about my day and my plans for the weekend. The tone of his voice was strained. Then he lay the bombshell on me. Cancer.

What he said after that, I couldn't remember. Details of the illness, what the Doctor had told him and his plans going forward. Nothing sunk in. I felt numb and my mind was a blank. A few minutes later he said he had to call my brother Rory as well. A task that couldn't have been easy. I told him that I would call him later. The phone went silent. They say your whole life can change in an instant. I finally comprehended what that meant.

My Dad now lies in the same bed, lively with conversation. A year earlier, he was bedridden with chronic back pains, where the cancer had spread. The two scenes could not be more different. He spent more than a month in my apartment, while my Mom ran errands and organised a new life where he could be comfortable and closer to a hospital. Where once he had been my rock and always looked after me, I was the one who had to take care of him before his treatment began. The roles had been reversed.

As a young boy, my Dad was my superhero, indestructible. A mountain among mortal men, who would fiercely protect and provide for his family. When I got older, I would always go to my Mom when I wanted anything or needed help with a problem. However, for more serious issues, my Dad is the one I would turn to. When I fell asleep on the sofa, he would be the one to carry me up the stairs to bed. For that month, I was the one to help him get to my bed and made sure he was comfortable, before I caught up on the latest boxset from my sleeper couch, in the living room.

To care for a parent is a humbling experience. Waking up in the middle of the night to help him with his medication. Tracking and logging his daily intake from a mountain of pills. Cooking. Cleaning. Staying with him until the agony from the pain subsided. He would spend most of the day in bed, or occasionally on his favourite spot on the sofa, unable to move because the discomfort would gnaw at him. Despite being a witness to the awful pain that he endured and the sleepless nights, I'd be forever grateful that I could at least return the favour for all the sacrifices he had made and for all the opportunities he provided for both Rory and I.

If you were to ask any member of his family, or any of his friends, they would all say the same when describing my Dad. The life of the party. He would never pass on an opportunity to do an impression or tell an anecdote (one I'd probably heard a hundred times before) that would have everyone roaring with laughter. The way that he could communicate with others was a special gift that very few people possess. He touched many lives, and those were richer for it. I remember a particularly bad night while he stayed with me. We were halfway through watching '12 Angry Men', and he decided to retire to bed as the pain was too intense. I sat by his side waiting for the morphine to kick in, speaking to him in an attempt to keep his mind off the stabbing pain. A few minutes later, something funny came up and we both laughed until we cried. Knowing my Dad, there will be many moments such as this throughout this book. There could not be a more fitting title than 'Laughter Through Tears'.

The months we lived together through those testing times brought us even closer together. I learnt a lot about him, not just as a father, but as a person. A risk taker and a dreamer. A person that only comes by, once in a generation. I sincerely hope that this book gives an insight into that individual and you enjoy the stories he chooses to share with the world.

From his spot on the bed he asks me if I'm hungry. I finish my notes on the speech and we head to the kitchen for some food.

"Do you want butter in your sandwiches" he asks

"No Dad, I don't like butter" I remind him for the thousandth time.

"Ok, no problem. I will still make you a great sandwich"

I've had to remind him for many, many years that I don't like butter, and I really hope that there are many, many years ahead that I can remind him again.

This book is dedicated to my wife Kim.
Every love story is beautiful, but ours is my favourite.

CHAPTER ONE
THE MEDALLION

I am sixty-five years old.

I was born and raised on an idyllic tropical island.

I am blessed with an incredible family and wonderful friends.

I have been married for thirty five years and I am still hopelessly in love.

I am a Dad and that is the greatest gift of all.

I have lived and worked on two Islands and three continents.

I have visited dozens of countries and discovered magical cities.

I am an entrepreneur and a risk taker.

I am adventurous and free spirited.

I have always dreamt big and laughed a lot.

I have lived a beautiful life with many stories to tell.

I have cancer.

Morning has broken. I wake, suddenly. A beacon of light has pierced through a gap in the black-out curtains, illuminating a tiny part of the darkened room. The dawning of each new day is important to me. A celebration, in fact. Today is the first day of a week's vacation in the South of France. Not a moment to waste. I swing both my legs over the side of the bed and slowly get to my feet. I feel stiff and ache all over. I look across at my wife. She is fast asleep. I get dressed as quietly as I can and leave the coolness of our air-conditioned bedroom.

I make my way to the kitchen, swallow a couple of painkillers and pour myself a large glass of fresh fruit juice. I slide open the large glass door, walk onto the terrace and for a good couple of seconds, close my eyes and take a deep breath. My senses tell me that I'm in Provence, the Alpes Maritime region to be precise. It is calm and tranquil and the delicious scent of lavender hangs in the air. The rented stone clad house is perched on a hilltop and overlooks a fantasy like scenery.

I walk cautiously along the edge of the swimming pool. I hear a buzzing sound. A swarm of dragonflies hover in mid-air, just above the surface of the pool water. I stand still and observe them for a long while. There is something magical about them. Bright rays from the rising sun filter through their transparent wings, sending a kaleidoscope of vivid colours shimmering on the water. To most humans, they are just irritating insects. Not to me, I have been fascinated by them from a very early age, always marvelling at their beauty and spectacular flying ability. Today I watch them very closely, admiring their gracefulness as they perform a precise and colourful aerial show, courtesy of nature.

At the end of the garden, past the pool, I find a bench perfectly positioned under the shade of a cypress tree. I sit, sipping my cold juice. I take in the stunning views of green hills and deep valleys that roll all the way down to the Mediterranean, dotted with stone clad dwellings, olive groves and purple patches of wild lavender. What a difference a year makes. On virtually the same day, a year ago, I was the unfortunate recipient of news that would change my life forever.

"You have cancer."

I sit still, feeling numb. I stare at the pathology report just handed me. It makes no sense. Words and numbers that are totally foreign to me. She repeats it again and it sounds more like an apology than a statement.

"You have cancer."

Three simple words which, once uttered, cannot be taken back. Three words which, within a split second of being spoken, turn your world upside down. Three words which, without judge or jury, hand you a life sentence. I cannot recall what my immediate reaction was on hearing these three words. Disbelief and a fair bit of anger, there were certainly no feelings or expressions of shock, grief or fear.

"Are you sure?" I question, looking across the desk at the young doctor. I had first consulted with her eighteen months ago, upon arriving back in South Africa. I needed regular check ups, and continuous prescriptions for my high blood pressure condition.

I recall taking an immediate liking to her. She was of Indian origin with an impossible surname to pronounce. From the very moment we met, she said that I reminded her of Mr Fawlty from the television series 'Fawlty Towers'. As my surname was just as complicated to pronounce as hers, she took to referring to me as Mr Fawlty, but in the nicest and most affectionate way. I, in turn called her Sybil. She had a lovely demeanour with a permanent smile on her face and we felt very comfortable in each other's company.

"Cancer" I repeat, now in total disbelief, "It cannot be, surely."

My previous consultations with her were for a chronic back pain. I was convinced, along with many others, that it was caused by the sciatica nerve. I began feeling this pain six months ago, and it gradually worsened. Every person who I came into contact with and who suffered from similar back pain assured me that it was indeed the sciatica nerve and that it would ease off after a period of time. Ease off, it did not. I was now taking painkillers and anti-inflammatories by the dozens for some sort of relief.

***

It all came to a head at the end of July 2016. On an early Friday evening, while watching the evening news with my wife, Kim, I felt nauseous. I swallowed a couple of anti-sickness tablets and went to bed early. Because of the pain, I could only lie on my back. As I was about to drift off to sleep, I felt an enormous stabbing pain at the bottom of my spine and down my left leg. I screamed in absolute agony and was soaked in a cold sweat by the time Kim arrived at my side. I told her the pain was extreme and that I was unable to move.

"I am calling the hospital" she cried out, seeing the state I was in. "They will need to send an ambulance."

"Not just yet," I reply, barely able to get the words out, "I've just remembered that because I took the anti-sickness pills, I forgot to take my other pills." I swallow a large dose of painkillers and anti-inflammatories and slowly the pain begins to recede. I still knew full well that what I had just experienced was clearly abnormal.

The next morning I call Sybil and she insists that I have x-rays done first thing on the Monday morning. She calls me back a few minutes later, giving me the time and the location of the radiologist, and also makes an appointment to see me the following day to discuss the results. I spend the rest of the weekend on my back in bed, hardly able to walk, struggling to even stand upright.

Thankfully by the time Monday morning comes, the pain has subsided enough, allowing me to get to the clinic and have the x-rays done. Following her instructions, they concentrate mainly on my lower back, spine and pelvic area. Meeting up with Sybil the next day, she gives me the good news that the x-rays revealed nothing serious, except a little arthritis at the bottom of the spine. She decides, however, that it is time to perform a series of blood tests, and takes various samples which are sent to the laboratory.

A couple of days later, a Thursday afternoon, I get a call from her surgery informing me that the results are in and the doctor wants me to call in as soon as I can.

"It's most probably my cholesterol" I tell Kim, walking out of our small simplex.

The doctor's surgery is only a five minute drive away. On entering the reception area, the young lady at the front desk tells me to go straight to the consulting room as the doctor is expecting me. Walking into the room, I notice straight away, that her usual 'smiley' facial expression has vanished.

"I know that this is the last thing you want to hear" she says softly, "I wish I had better news, I'm so, so sorry. Your blood results reveal a PSA level of 247, this is enormously high" she explains. "Normally a PSA reading of 7 to 8 indicates that you have prostate cancer, your high level suggests that it may be spreading."

At this point, she kindly reaches forward and softly cradles my hands that I had unknowingly turned into fists. She purposefully remains silent, allowing me enough time to regain my composure. A mixture of strange and dreadful emotions run through my mind.

"What do I do now?" I hear myself asking her, hardly recognising the sound of my own voice.

"You need to see a Urologist, urgently" she pauses.

"I will write you a note, take that along with your blood results. Would you like me to refer you to someone?"

"Let me discuss it with my family first," I reply. "I am sure they know someone."

"I am imploring you, you need to do this urgently, not a single day to waste."

On leaving the room, she gives me an amiable handshake. I see sadness and sympathy in her face, and it adds to my growing anxiety.

I step out of her surgery, armed with her note and blood results. It is a warm and sunny late afternoon in Durban North. It suddenly dawns on me that this is the first time since we met that she did not refer to me as Mr Fawlty.

"This must be flipping serious," I mutter to myself.

I was about to make my way back to the car, when I remembered that Kim had asked me to grab a loaf of bread and a litre of milk from the grocery store. Cancer or not, life goes on. I limp into the supermarket located alongside the surgery. Feeling numb and robotic, I slowly make my way up the aisle towards the cold storage.

"Hey Gilly!" I recognise the voice instantly. It is an old school friend of mine. We had met again after a period of over forty years at a school class reunion. I had hardly recognised him. He had doubled in size, and that's horizontally. Since the reunion, we kept bumping into each other at the store. He lived just up the road from us. A good and jolly person.

"Hello Johnny" I greet him with a smile, trying to sound as casual as I can. There is no way that I was going to share and discuss my disastrous news with him.

" What's with the limping?" He enquires, having obviously seen me stumble into the supermarket.

"Nothing serious," I lie. "Just been to the doctor next door, it's sciatica."

"Ouch, that's painful. I know all about it." He says, grimacing.

It is official then, the whole city's population, has at one stage or another suffered from sciatica. Before I have the chance to tell him that I'm in a hurry, he moves onto his favourite subject.

"So what do you think of our Blitzbokkers, my broer?" He asks proudly, puffing out his enormous chest. "They are giving everyone a serious klap."

Here we go, I thought. Only a few seconds in the conversation and we're discussing rugby. I was definitely in no mood to stand and get a lecture on the wonders of South African rugby. I needed to nip this in the bud.

"Well and good for the Blitzbokkers," I reply, pausing a while before delivering the killer blow. "But pity about the Bokkes. Getting beaten by the likes of Ireland and Japan, not good is it, what's happening?"

The moment the words leave my mouth I felt a little guilty. Running down the mighty Springboks was a no, no in this part of the world. But it worked. The broad smile vanished from his even broader face and I could almost hear the rattling in his brain, searching for a suitable reply in defence of his adored Boks, but nothing came, except;

"Sorry, I must shoot, Broer, no time to chat today. The missus is waiting in the bakkie and the aircon is not working. She must be melting."

With that, he slaps me on the back and walks away towards the check-outs. I stand there, holding onto a bottle of half-skimmed milk, in great agony. The pain from the 'friendly' slap is unbearable as it travels down my spine to the pelvic area. Well deserved, I thought, for being otherwise. After giving myself a little time to recover, I pick up a loaf of bread, pay for the items and make my way to the car park. I look around and am very relieved to find no trace of Johnny, the bakkie and the melted missus.

I sit in the car for a fairly long time, contemplating how to break this disastrous news to my wife. I watch the people in the busy car park, going about their business and everyday life, distant and oblivious of my turmoil. I have been, in the past half an hour or so, cast out of that life. A life that I enjoyed to the fullest had been dealt a severe blow. I am now a cancer sufferer with the clear possibility of an early death.

As I insert the key in the ignition socket, I hold on tightly to the medallion at the end of the keyring. The medallion depicts the image of Pope John Paul on the one side and the image of the Sacred Heart on the other. I had purchased it on a trip to the Vatican over twenty years ago and it was blessed by the Pope. I always carried it on me and whenever there was a dark moment in my life, I held onto it and prayed for guidance.

I sit there, gently caressing my medallion. I feel trapped and confused.

"Surely this is not happening to me. It's seriously crazy."

Suddenly a calmness comes over me. Something deep inside me tells me to get a hold of myself. You can beat this, no matter how bad the diagnosis or how far it has spread. You can beat this. Right there and then, I decide to declare war on this hideous disease. A strange and gentle feeling envelope me as I start the car and drive out of the busy car park.

CHAPTER TWO
LAUGHTER THROUGH TEARS

The short drive home gives me a chance to prepare myself and gather my thoughts before breaking the awful news to my wife. Being told that you have cancer is bad enough, but now having to share this unbearable diagnosis with loved ones and family would be enormously difficult. I was anxious over how Kim would deal with it. We were about to embark on an extremely tough journey. The unknown really. Trying times ahead.

"Thought you got lost" she says smiling, meeting me at the door." Did you go somewhere else after the doctor's?"

"No, I bumped into Johnny at the store." I reply, handing her the shopping bag.

"I have some bad news, Darling." I say, feeling a lump beginning to form at the back of my throat.

I was not going to beat around the bush. There was no other way to go about this.

"What is it?" She asks anxiously, holding my hand as we sit on the settee. "Please don't tell me that Johnny has asked us around and you've said yes?"

"I have prostate cancer," I blurt out, "and the doctor thinks it may have spread to other parts of my body. It could be serious."

The colour drains from her pretty face.

"Prostate cancer." She repeats, shaking her head and looking greatly confused." From a sore back? Surely not."

She moves closer to me, holding both of my hands. An empty, sympathetic look in her eyes.

"How can it be prostate cancer?" She questions. "Surely there should have been some indication when you empty your bladder, or some sort of bleeding?"

"Not necessarily, I'm told." I give her a little time for the news to sink in. I wrap my arms around her and hold her gently.

She lays her head on my shoulder and we both start crying. We hug and cry softly for a few awful minutes.

"You cannot leave me now." She whispers through her tears. "We have so much to look forward to. What am I going to do without you in my life? What are the boys going to do without you?"

"No need to worry," I reply with as much positivity as I can muster, wiping the tears away. "You really don't think that I'm going to let that effing cancer beat me - do you?"

The words had no sooner left my mouth, that we both burst out in laughter. It was nervous laughter, but laugh we did, still hugging each other. Throughout our married life, we've always managed to laugh through our tears. That shared laughter has been a part of our journey from the moment we met. A strong, magical and healing experience.

"You are right. I know you too well. You will fight and beat this." She says, holding on to me. "You've always overcome obstacles and you know that the boys and I will be by your side every step of the way."

And that was that. The hard part was out of the way. We dried our tears and I genuinely felt that I had already shown too much respect to that awful disease. It has picked on the wrong person this time. I clearly knew that I was about to face the hardest test of my life, but I have never hesitated to put up a good fight before. And I have not lost many, even in the most difficult of circumstances.

"There is not a moment to waste." I tell Kim. "I need to speak to Don before I do anything else. Do you think he will answer his phone at this time of the day? Maybe send him a message and ask him to contact us urgently."

Don, my brother in law, is a highly respected Radiologist in the state of Florida. He uses imaging technology to diagnose disease and offers advice to Doctors and Specialists for treatment of the same. He works from home and I had the pleasure of watching him go about his trade on a couple of occasions. His study resembles an air traffic control station, with his desk surrounded by five large monitors, connected to various hospitals from different States. He is soft spoken, well educated and most importantly a very good friend of mine. He was the perfect person to talk to and get sound advice from. Within a few minutes of Kim sending the message, the phone rings. It's him.

"Hi Boet," He sounds concerned. "Is there a problem?"

"Sorry to trouble you Don, I know it's very early morning there." I feel my voice beginning to crack up again. "I have some bad news."

I proceed to tell him about my visit to the Doctor and read the blood test results out to him. All the while, he remains silent, listening intently until I finish.

"Gosh, I did not expect this." He says softly, pauses a short while. Then in his usual self-assured way goes on, "your PSA level is exceedingly high. At that level, chances are that the cancer has spread, but we won't know that for sure until all the tests and scans are done."

"All I can tell you Gil," he carries on, "is that if I had cancer and was given the choice of which type I could have, I would choose prostate cancer. It's the least aggressive of all cancers."

"Having said that," he continues, "your back pain is a major concern and you must be seen by a Urologist as soon as possible. My advice to you is to get back to the UK urgently, within the next couple of days if possible," he urges. "Both Ryan and Rory are in Bristol and from what I've heard, the Bristol Urological Institute prides itself with some of the best Specialists in the country, if not the world. Get Kim to book you on a flight soonest. I would not even entertain the idea of seeing a Urologist in Durban. They will be wasting precious time with all sorts of tests." he says, and then reminds me: "You do remember what happened to Dad fifteen years ago?"

I remember only too well. His Dad, my Father in Law, was on holiday in the states, visiting both his sons. On a Sunday morning, while staying with Don and getting ready to go to church, he felt unwell and collapsed, bringing up a huge amount of blood. Fortunately, Don was on hand to stabilise him until the ambulance arrived. It probably saved his life. After a series of tests were carried out, he was diagnosed with cancer of the oesophagus. The tumour had burst and the only way forward was for him to undergo immediate surgery. The affected section of his oesophagus had to be removed urgently. Even though his Dad had travel insurance that would cover the medical costs of the procedure in the United States, Don felt it would be best for him to fly back to the UK for surgery. A good few people raised their eyebrows at that suggestion, including myself, but it turned out to be the correct call.

After spending a couple of days regaining his strength, my Father in law flew back to the UK and soon afterwards underwent surgery at the Royal Gwent Hospital in Newport. It was a major operation and he spent weeks in the intensive care unit. After a seriously long and difficult period at the hospital, he recovered fully. Today at the ripe old age of eighty-eight, he and my Mother in law have moved to Florida, enjoying life and the sunshine to the fullest.

At the end of my phone conversation with Don, I hang up, telling him that I would discuss everything with Kim and thanked him for his wise and encouraging words. Shortly after the phone call, he emails me a bunch of information. It's about the Bristol Urological Institute. They are based in Southmead, just North of the city centre. It is the largest urological centre in the country and boasts a team of leading Urologists and Researchers, who are at the forefront of prostate cancer care in the UK. If my mind was not already made up, it was most certainly made up now.

"I think Don is right," I tell Kim. "I feel significantly better after chatting to him."

"The sooner I leave, the better." I explain. "I can go on ahead of you, the boys will take good care of me."

"There's a lot to discuss." Kim declares. "Let's have a cuppa, it will clear our minds."

She hugs me and goes to the kitchen. I get up cautiously and painfully walk out to the small patio and swimming pool area. My back still hurts, but now, at long last, I know the reason why.

I look up at the African sky. It's early evening and there is not a cloud in sight. As per usual at that precise time of day, a flock of seagulls appear from nowhere, their whitish bodies silhouetted against the clear blue sky. They squawk furiously as they fly over me, in a V formation, making their way to the sea. I watch as they glide without a single wing beat, gracefully swaying from side to side. Their sharp squawks are acknowledged by a bunch of large Hadeda birds who always gathered in a tall tree at the back of our garden at this exact time of day. They respond back to the seagulls in their extremely loud and distinctive call. A daily cacophony of deafening sound that always played on my nerves and drove me crazy. But not today, inexplicably, the 'racket' soothes me. A message of hope, perhaps. But it was more than that. A sudden and clear indication that there are much more important things in life than letting a perfectly trivial and natural act become an annoyance.

"Tea's ready, Darling." Kim calls out from the patio door.

For just a few minutes, these birds thankfully blurred my thoughts away from the trauma and the horrendous journey that I knew laid ahead of us.

"What do we do with all our personal belongings and furniture?" Kim asks.

That's the woman I loved and admired. While I was out, bird watching, she was already planning the way forward. Sitting having our tea, she sets out the details.

"Let's get you to Bristol asap." She says. "I will try and book a flight for early next week. No point in sending all the furniture, I will try to sell the lot here. We have no idea where we will end up anyway. I will pack our personal stuff and all items of sentimental value in boxes and have them stored until we decide what to do with them. Hopefully I will be able to achieve all that in a couple of weeks and then I'll join you."

It was barely ninety minutes or so, since I was told I had cancer, and we had already given up on all of our future plans and dreams and replaced them with tough and life changing decisions, all made in a calm, positive and decisive way. A good start.

We then discussed when and how we would break the news to our two sons, knowing all too well how devastating it would be for them. You always remember being given bad news, no matter how well it is delivered. I wanted to be well prepared and mentally focussed before speaking to them. They had already sent Whatsapp messages to their Mother asking for news of the blood tests. We decided that we would call them the following day, being Friday. We knew that Ryan's girlfriend, Lauren, was driving up from London to spend the weekend with him, so he would not be on his own. Rory, the youngest of the two, lived with his longterm girlfriend, Elinor.

While I was on the phone with Don, my niece, Mylene, who lived in the same complex, had called to find out about the test results. She was devastated on hearing the news and decided to drive to her Mother's house to tell her. My sister, Marielle, was the closest to me by nature of birth, out of nine siblings. We enjoyed a very special relationship and spoke to each other on a daily basis. Her daughter knew that breaking such unexpected and sad news to her had to be done in a compassionate manner.

The moment that news of my illness began circulating, we were instantly inundated with phone calls and visits. The bad news was made worse when we told them that we were leaving Durban immediately and going back home to the UK. The visits from family lasted until late that first evening and were at times very trying and emotional, with an enormous amount of tears and hugs being shared, as well as wonderful words of support. Knowing me well, they were all united in the belief that I would defeat this monstrous disease. By the time the last visitor left, I felt completely drained and in a lot of pain. After taking an above normal dose of painkillers, I laid on my back in the dark bedroom, processing the thought of how our lives and future plans had changed course completely.

As the news spread, the phone kept ringing. At the end of each call, Kim would come to the bedroom, telling me who it was and passing on their good wishes. One such call was from my niece Francoise, who lived in Canada. When Kim told her that I was flying back to the UK for urgent treatment, she spontaneously offered her free air miles so that I could get bumped up and have the comfort of travelling first class. That was the type of kind gesture and support I could expect from my family.

That first night, was arguably the worst night of my life. I laid there, drifting in and out of a nightmarish sleep, due in part to the amount of medication I was taking. I knew that my precious wife lying next to me was also hurting as much as I was. I also knew that we've always been a tower of strength for each other in the face of adversity. I will fight and win this battle, I kept reassuring myself. We have too much to live for; an abundance of love, happiness and still many naughty adventures ahead of us. With that in mind, I drift off to sleep.

I wake, and the first thing that crosses my mind is that today is the day I would be breaking the awful news to my sons. Not something I was looking forward to, especially by long distance phone calls. A feeling of utter sadness and despondency comes over me, knowing full well the enormous hurt it would cause. I had to do it in the gentlest way. Family and friends popped in and out during the course of the day, showering us with love and support. The last visitor leaves and it is time to make the dreaded calls, it was around seven in the evening, their time.

I call Ryan, the eldest, first and then Rory. On hearing my voice, the first thing they do is enquire about the blood results. Kim had messaged them, saying we were hoping to hear from the doctor's room this afternoon. I try to sound as upbeat and as calm as I can. I inform them that the results revealed that I have prostate cancer, which is in most cases, treatable, as long as it was done urgently. I went on telling them that on Don's advice, I was returning to the UK as soon as possible for treatment and that Bristol, where they both lived, was the ideal location for the best possible care.

Their reaction to the phone calls were almost identical. It began with shock and the same sad expression of "Oh, no

Dad." And at the end of our chat, both agreed that I needed to get back to Bristol urgently and that I would be taken good care of. Towards the end of the calls, I could feel that they were getting upset as the news began to sink in. I told them we would stay in touch and I would let them know my travel arrangement and I was super excited that I would be seeing them real soon.

On hanging up, I tell Kim that I thought they took the news as well as can be expected, but at the same time, I knew they were hurting. I look up, and find her eyes filled with tears. I hug her and feel a sting at the back of my eyes. No crying now, I quietly scold myself. I try desperately to find something funny to say, but on this occasion nothing comes to mind. There would be no laughter through tears on this occasion. Instead, we sit, in silence, thinking of our boys many, many miles away, wishing we could be with them, comforting them.

Many months later, I question both of them on how they reacted receiving that phone call. Ryan said he did not want to revisit that evening, as it was too painful. I learnt that Rory took the call as he was about to enter a pub where a bunch of his friends were waiting for him. Instead, he went back home, calling Elinor, who had also gone out with her friends and asked her to meet him back at their flat, as he had received some very sad news.

On reaching home, he noticed messages from his friends at the pub, enquiring his whereabouts.

"Where are you, mate? We are all waiting." They had enquired.

"Sorry, guys," he replied. "I can't make it tonight."

"What do you mean?" They insisted. "You're double-parked here!" Meaning that there were already two drinks on the bar waiting for him.

"Why can't you make it?"

"I've just heard my Dad has cancer." He replied, turning his phone off.

CHAPTER THREE
CIRCLE OF STRENGTH

Every family has a story to tell, especially a large Mauritian family. Welcome to mine.

I have benefited enormously from growing up in a large family. Growing up as the youngest sibling, I have always had a great support system. It made me self reliant, independent and also made me understand the real meaning of responsibility. I mentioned in the previous chapter that we were a family of nine, made up of six boys and three girls. It was in fact a family of eleven, but sadly my parents lost two of their children, both boys and both at an early age. I will discuss that at a later stage. I also need to point out at this stage that my Dad Joseph, married twice. His first wife, Raymonde, very sadly passed away before her time, leaving my Dad and his five young children grief stricken and disconsolate. He had lost someone he had never dreamt of losing, but fortunately he soon found love again in the form of my mother, Yolande. She was at the time engaged to his younger brother. Yes, I know, but such things do happen, especially on a small Island, and it turned out to be a wonderful marriage that would last a lifetime.

Being a stepmother to five young children was no doubt a particularly difficult and challenging role for my Mother to assume. Knowing the sorrow and pain that her step-children had endured, she loved and brought them up as her own. At the same time, she began having children of her own. We were all brought up as one family and I could not have chosen better siblings. Not once did I ever look upon, or think of my older siblings, as 'half' or 'step'. To me they were simply my family and I had as much love and affection for them as I did for the rest. My siblings will always remain my best friends. The choice of having such a large family meant sacrifices had to be made, but along with it came much happiness too. We squabbled, laughed and cried together, and the many memories we made is what bonded us so close together. I remember from an early age being routinely called the wrong name by my parents. I accepted that they had a long list of names to remember, and it usually took a while to eventually get to mine, so I learnt to answer to whatever version of my name they came up with. I also ended up with many charming nicknames, such as Tresor, Zoulou, Dioul.

Having to bring up nine children, discipline was high on my parents agenda. They were both severe, but fair. They certainly believed in the dreadful concept of 'if you save the rod, you spoil the child' and had no hesitation of practising it. All my brothers and I grew up knowing that if we dared step out of line, physical punishment was a guarantee. In those days, children were seen and not heard, especially at the dining table. To put it all into context, I need to share this little episode with you. I was about eleven years old, and at dinner one evening, I asked permission to tell a joke. My Dad stared at me with his steely blue eyes, his spectacles on the bridge of his nose, and after debating for a while whether it was a wise idea, he gave me the go ahead.

"What would you call a forest without birds?" I asked enthusiastically.

Everyone at the table thought about it for a while, but no one could come up with an answer.

"It's the hair growing under Marielle's armpit!" I declared triumphantly.

With that, poor Marielle, who had just reached puberty, howled in agony. With her being my Dad's blue eyed girl, I immediately realised my awful faux pas, but it was too late. I was dragged from the dining room by my now furious Father and was given a hiding all the way to my bedroom with his trusted 'rotin'. I had to remain there for the rest of the evening, without anything to eat or drink. For the consideration of some sensitive readers that may think this was far too harsh a punishment, I will not get into the details of what happened if one came home with bad grades. Oh yes, a 'rotin', was either a length of bamboo or a thin stick, shaped from a branch obtained from a nearby tree, and if it happened to break on you, which it often did, you were given the privilege of being the one to cultivate another one for the next hiding.

By nature of the age gaps, I grew up in totally different decades to my siblings. I, for that reason, had stronger bonds with the ones closest to me, those being Micheline, Christian and Marielle. As children we grew up on a sugar plantation estate at Montagne Longue, situated on the northern side of Mauritius. We enjoyed a peaceful, stress free life. Unfortunately, the same cannot be said for my older siblings; Josee, Michel, Jacques, Cecil and Henri. Our parents had gone through some very difficult times, both before and after the war. Life was hard, and I remember very clearly the sad stories told to me by my Parents as well as my sister, Josee, of the enormous hardships they had endured, on a daily basis.

A very trying period for them occurred when my Dad took up a job as resident manager on the tiny island of Agalega. Agalega, a territory dependent of the Mauritian Republic, is an archipelago of two tiny islands situated about a thousand kilometres North of Mauritius. My Dad's duty was to manage the two Islets and their population of about two hundred locals. The economic existence of the Islets depended primarily on the export of coconut oil and salt fish to Mauritius. The only connection to Mauritius was by sea. A ship bringing provisions and collecting cargo called only once per month, and as there was no functional port or harbour, the ship would cast anchor half a kilometre from the coast in deep sea. The cargo would then be loaded and offloaded by means of small wooden boats called pirogues.

There was no running water on the Islets, and electricity was limited to a few hours per evening, supplied by a generator running on diesel. This is where my family spent many years. Other 'outsiders' on the Islets, were a Health Officer come Pharmacist, that provided medical care; a Midwife; an Assistant Manager and a Meteorologist. At the tender age of Sixteen, my sister Josee fell in love with and married the Meteorologist. The wedding took place at the small Chapel on the island and all of the Locals turned up. Something else happened on these Islets. Something just as beautiful. But that is for another chapter.

Having honoured his work contract in Agalega, my Dad returned to Mauritius, where he eventually found work on the sugar estate I referred to earlier. He was offered a good position, being the accountant and basically second in charge. I was born a couple of years prior to that, and grew up in a charming colonial home on the estate, surrounded by an orchard that boasted an abundance of tropical fruit trees. We even had a river that meandered at the bottom of the property. Life was very good. However, during that same period my older siblings, led by Josee and her husband Francis, were lured by the promise of a better and brighter future in South Africa. So, one by one, they left the Island to make a new life for themselves on the African Continent. Eventually, only my Parents and the four younger siblings from the second bed remained on the Island.

I have often told my sons how I wish they could have experienced the same wonderful upbringing which I enjoyed up until my teenage years in Mauritius. Life was carefree. Christian, Marielle and I spent long, lazy days playing in the orchard, climbing up tall trees and swimming in the river. We would spend our school holidays at various beach cottages dotted along the coastline, and spent dawn to dusk in the clear lagoons. We snorkeled, fished with spear guns and often swam out to the reefs.

The years rolled on, until my sister Micheline, having visited her brothers and sister in Durban, decided that she also wanted to emigrate. Christian indicated that he would be the next to follow. This all took place during a period of uncertainty in Mauritius. The Island, which was under British rule, had begun a campaign for it's independence. A referendum on independence was held in the early sixties, and the contest was overwhelmingly won by a pro-independence coalition. This led to a period of communal strife on the Island between anti and pro independent parties, which resulted in a period of intense violence, causing many deaths. This period of tension and uncertainty of an independent Mauritius without the backing of the British, as well as the fear of being separated from all of their children, were reasons enough for my Parents to make the very brave and difficult decision to leave the Island

and emigrate to South Africa themselves. Mauritius went on to gain independence in 1968, and it's first Prime Minister was a medical practitioner named, Seewoosagar Ramgoolam. The island, after a few difficult years, prospered. Today, with a diversified economy based on tourism, textiles, sugar and more recently, financial and information technology, is the only sub-Saharan country to have shown economic resilience, growth and stability.

We landed in Durban, South Africa, in the winter of 1965. I was thirteen years old and could hardly speak a word of English. I remember that day vividly. We were welcomed at the airport by all of our siblings and their own families. It was a joyous occasion for all of us to be reunited again after many years. My older brothers and sisters felt like total strangers to me, having last seen them when I was just a mere toddler. Josee's four children were in the same age bracket as myself, Marielle and Christian. I was an uncle twice before I was born and became a great, great uncle in my fifties. My brothers Michel and Jacques were now also married. As the years passed, all of my brothers and sisters, one by one, married and had children. I was the last to marry, and the year was 1975.

The family grew larger and larger. Our parents instilled in us the importance of family get-togethers and we met frequently, which strengthened our bond. Love, understanding and security, all packaged together is how our family bond was formed, like a safe harbour. We shared and celebrated many joyous occasions, such as birthdays, weddings, baptisms and Christmases.

Sadly however, being part of such a large and growing family brought its fair share of losses and tragedies. We lost our Mother to cancer. She was only sixty one years old. Her passing had a profound effect on me and my siblings and left a huge void in all our lives. We were concerned how our Father would cope without her, but with the love and support of his children, he went on to live to a ripe old age.

Tragedy after tragedy struck our family at regular intervals. These were dark times and not something I would like to write about, except to say that two of my brothers and their wives lost their sons, both wonderful young men in their prime. My sister lost two of her grandchildren, the teenage daughters of my nephews. Just recently, one of my niece's son, was stillborn. These were all shattering experiences to the parents, causing intense anguish and heartbreak and forcing them on an indescribable journey of sorrow and survival. It is rightly said that you don't know what love is until you've carried a child, and you don't know what pain is until you've lost a child. No truer words spoken. One thing they could always count on however, was the never ending gentle words of comfort and support from our very special family. We were and will always remain, a powerful circle of strength.

CHAPTER FOUR
WHITE SAND TO WHITE SNOW

Under the unforgivingly hot, tropical Mauritian sun, we diligently followed my sister Josee along the back roads of Curepipe, the Island's second largest city. She and her daughter, Francoise, were visiting Kim and I on the Island. They were spending a couple of weeks and staying with us at the home we had rented at Le Morne, which was situated on the Southeast side of the Island. We had zig-zagged the area by car for a good half an hour, but failed to find the location of the house she was eager to show me. It was the house she and her husband Francis lived in and the reason for showing it to me was because I was born there, in their front room.

We decided to park the car and continue the search on foot. She felt it may trigger her memory. Walking a few paces behind her, I was amazed how fit and well preserved she looked for a woman of eighty-three years of age, always perfectly groomed and smartly dressed. Suddenly she came to an abrupt halt.

"Voila!" She shouted excitedly in her mother tongue. "I have found it. This is the house."

We caught up to her and stood at the corner of a curb, staring at an abandoned little house, wrapped in overgrown shrubs.

"Well done, Josee!" I said enthusiastically, wrapping my arms around her.

"It was a beautiful house, full of love," she went on. "And it had a neat bamboo hedge around it."

She pointed to a fairly large, glassless steel framed window, situated at the centre of the house.

"That's the room you were born in, my boy." She said happily. "That was over sixty years ago and I was at that time pregnant with Francoise. She was born a couple of months later."

And here we were, Francoise and I, over six decades later, looking at where our life had begun. The four of us stood there for a long while, in happy silence.

As a young teenager, life in South Africa was to prove to be very different to the one I enjoyed so much in Mauritius. For instance, when I left the island, I was one of only two white people in our classroom. My best friends at school were made up mainly of Indian and Chinese lads. I was now thrust into a whites only, boys school where most of the students seemed to have been overfed and were subsequently far too big for their age. I had difficulty putting a sentence together in my broken English, and that quickly introduced me to bullying.

Bullying was a sordid sort of pastime in those days. The bullies would operate in groups of three or more and made sure that their victims were smaller and physically weaker than them, hence negating a physical encounter. They would pick on you if you were skinny, wore glasses, had red hair and so on. Because of my accent and slight build, I was a perfect target. Three of my classmates decided to pick on me and make my life miserable. They nicknamed me 'Frenchie' and abused me verbally on a daily basis. These cowards would always do their bullying in front of an audience, where they would be proud recipients of cheers and laughter at my expense. Bad news for them is that they picked on the wrong person, there was no way I was going to tolerate such treatment and let these brutes get away with it. I had a plan.

We had just moved into a house in the area and my school was situated a couple of kilometres away. It took me roughly twenty minutes to cycle there on my new bike. My parents employed what was in those days referred to as a 'garden boy', who lived in and worked as our gardener. His name was Bennett, a powerfully built, young Zulu man. He became my best friend. We spent most afternoons after school playing football on the beach, which was within walking distance from where we lived. We also spent many hours cycling around the suburb we lived in, North of Durban. He would sit on the crossbar and pedal furiously, while I sat on the saddle. We would take turns, him doing the uphills and me the downhills.

I found out where the three bullies lived and one afternoon after school, Bennett and I paid each one of them a visit. I went up to their front door and called them out. I introduced Bennett to them, having schooled him to glare at them with that vicious grimace he could muster. I warned them that if they ever dared bully me again, Bennett and I would be back and they would be made to regret it. The first two, being without their back ups and seeing Bennett's size, apologised and hurried back into their homes. The third tyrant however, did not enjoy being threatened and as we cycled away, ran behind us and threw a stone. I ducked just in time and the projectile smacked poor Bennett at the back of his head. That made him furious. He turned the bike around and we caught up with the fleeing offender as he reached his driveway. Without going into any details, it is suffice to say that he was made to regret throwing that stone. Cycling home that evening, we stopped at the local store and bought a couple of cold drinks to celebrate and have a good laugh. It was mission accomplished. From that day onwards, I was never teased or bullied at school again.

Stored at the back of my mind and linked with the good memories I have of Bennett, I have another good story to tell. Also employed by my parents was an elderly African lady by the name of Alice. She was employed as the 'domestic servant'. Alice, like Bennett, had her sleeping quarters at the bottom level of the house alongside the garage. Much to my Mother's anguish, Alice performed her duties at a snail's pace. As she could not speak English, My Mom resorted to either sign language, or me as the interpreter, to relate to Alice that she was much too slow. These were her only ways of communication. Neither worked, Alice did things her own way, and that was that. However, there was one activity she excelled at and it was a very well kept secret between her, Bennett and I. She was a master brewer.

She had partitioned off a corner of her room and set up a 'homemade' distillery for the production of 'shimiyane'. It consisted of a primus stove and various glass tubes and jars. Shimiyane is an intoxicating home-brewed drink made from sugar and water. It was banned due to its high alcohol content. This did not deter Alice one bit. She produced a good few litres per week and once bottled, Bennett would use my bike and deliver the goods to eager customers, all domestic servants like herself. She made a tidy profit and Bennett, being the logistic manager, received his fair share. I was very happy and excited that they trusted me enough to involve me in their private little venture.

Often, on Saturday afternoons, I would meet up with some of my school mates and go to our local cinema. This particular Saturday, 'The Party' with Peter Sellers was showing and I had been looking forward to seeing it. As per usual, Bennett would cycle up with me to the town centre, do some deliveries and then pick me up after the show. Sadly, because of the colour of his skin and the horrid rules of Apartheid, he was not allowed in the cinema. For some reason, it is something we never discussed. It was an accepted way of life, and I was fortunate to be on the right side of this vile system.

I got dressed, went down and knocked on Bennett's door, but there was no answer. On entering the room, I found him passed out on the bed and no amount of shaking would wake him. It was obvious that he and Alice took part in a product tasting session earlier on. I was now going to miss the show and I was furious. I needed to teach him a lesson. As it was Guy Fawkes season, I grabbed a pack of 'Tom Thumbs' firecrackers from my room, undid the pack and laid it length wise on his chest, which was smartly dressed in a new Lacoste style shirt. I lit the fuse and walked out. Running up the steps to the house, I realised the stupidness of my action, but it was too late. As I entered the lounge from the balcony, I heard the loud, machine gun type noise as the tiny fire crackers exploded.

"What was that?" my Dad enquired as I entered the house.

"I Don't know." I replied, now very concerned. Total silence followed the explosion. Surely he could not have slept through that.

A few seconds later, there was a knock at the backdoor. I cringed as my Mom opened the top half of the stable door. There stood Bennett, naked chested and holding on to his smouldering shirt. The skin on his torso had turned pink. My

Mom, in her self-styled sign language, asked him what had happened to his shirt. He pointed directly at me. Both of my Parents turned around, staring at me open mouthed. In turn, I also turned round but found no one behind me. My sense of humour and lack of sympathy towards poor Bennett did not go down well with them. I was gated for a couple of weeks and had to replace the shirt from the little money I had saved. Bennett sulked for a couple of days, but soon all was well again and we carried on with our adventures.

The years moved on and while still at high school, my sisters Micheline and Marielle and my brother Christian got married. My parents sold the house and we moved into an apartment in the city centre. The buyers of the house had decided to hire both Alice and Bennett. Moving day was a sad day for me, saying goodbye to them. I promised I would keep in touch.

Weeks turned into months, until one afternoon after school I decided to surprise them with a visit. The house was a thirty minute walk from the school. On reaching it, I could hardly recognise the front garden. It looked manicured, with fresh flower beds on each side of the long driveway. Walking up to the house, I noticed that all of the windows and doors were shut and assumed that there was nobody at home.

Feeling disappointed, I began walking away when I heard a familiar sound coming from the back garden. It was Alice singing one of her favourite Zulu songs.

She was busy hanging the laundry on the windy drier and stopped dead in her tracks when she saw me coming around the side of the house.

"I'm so, so happy to see you." She cried, and wrapped me in her arms.

"I'm very happy to see you too Alice." I replied, looking around for Bennett to appear from somewhere.

"How is Bennett?" I asked. "Where is he?"

"His Father passed away last month." She said. "He has gone back to the family farm to help his Mother. He is not coming back."

"So sorry to hear that." I reply. "That explains why the garden is looking so neat."

With that, we both explode in laughter.

But soon, a sadness envelopes me. I knew I would probably never see Bennett again.

We chatted for a long while. she told me that she had stopped her home brewing - it was getting too risky. She also wanted to stop work and go back to her children and grandchildren on the farm. She walked with me to the end of the driveway. I hugged her and promised to visit again. Sadly, I never did.

***

A couple of years later, I matriculate from high school with good grades and a university exemption. My parents could not afford to send me to university and that suited me just fine. The five years spent in high school instilled a great amount of self-confidence and work ethic in me. I considered myself both streetwise and smart enough to face the world and get on in life. My Dad told me that he was pleased with my results and gave me some money to cover my bus fare to the city centre so that I could begin a job search. The very next day, I was offered a position by the recruiting officer of the first institution I walked into. It was Barclays Bank. I began work the following day and remember clearly spending half of my first month wages on long playing vinyls of my music idol, Cat Stevens. Within the first year of starting work and with my Dad's help, I purchased my first car, a toyota corolla.

I worked at the bank for three years, progressing from junior clerk, to telling and then to the foreign exchange department. A wise man then suggested to me that a career at the bank was a monument for security but a graveyard for ambition. With that in mind and a yearning to get into sales and retail, I resigned from the bank and joined a large furniture retailer. I started off as an assistant manager, but quickly moved up the management ladder, ending up being in charge of the flagship store within a few years. The store did extremely well and I was rewarded with numerous awards, one being a fully paid month's holiday to the East, visiting Thailand, Hong Kong and Singapore.

It was during that period that I met and married my first wife. We were both much too young and the marriage never worked and only lasted a couple of years. The only good thing that came out of it was the birth of my daughter, Chantal. Also during that same period, we lost our Mother after a long and brave battle with cancer. She was only sixty-one years old and her passing was a huge blow to me and all of my siblings. I was very close to her.

It was a year or so later that I met the love of my life. It was Gold cup day, a major event on the South African horse racing calendar. I went to the race course with a good friend of mine and we met up with some of my brothers and sisters and their spouses. After the day's racing, we decided to go for a meal at a steakhouse situated on the beachfront. We had just been shown to our tables and whilst going through the menu, I first set eye on her. Straight long blonde hair cascaded down her shapely figure, all the way down past her waist. She was waiting on a table not far from ours and I assumed rightly that she was a student doing part time work, waitressing.

A sculptor could not have fashioned her beautiful facial features any better. I watched her every move and there was something inexplicably special about her. I now needed to be bold and engage her in conversation. As she walked past our table I stood up, blocking her passage and introduced myself, before politely asking her what her name was.

"Kim." She replied, looking seriously bemused. "What can I do for you?"

"I would like your phone number, please." I asked cheekily. "You are very pretty and I would like to take you out on a date."

She stared at me for a while, clearly astonished. She then smiled, shook her head, brushed past me and carried on with her duties.

As I sat down, my amiable friend was busy laughing his head off.

"Her phone number." He bellowed. "My friend, you're batting way out of your league."

"She is much too young and far too beautiful for you." He went on, howling with laughter.

Once he had sufficiently calmed down, I tell him in a very calm and assured tone,

"Laugh all you want my friend, but you've just met my future wife."

Kim and I married four years later in 1983, but not before a little struggle. Her parents, being staunch Catholics, were desperately unhappy with their precious daughter dating a divorced man. We had to wait until her 21st birthday to announce our engagement. As the Catholic church does not recognise divorce and to keep peace with her parents, we were married in the registry office. This was much to my chagrin, as I knew that Kim's dream was to walk down that aisle in a wedding dress, and what a walk that would have been. Nonetheless she looked like a princess on our wedding day, in an amazing dress hand made by my sister Micheline. Our reception was held under a marquee, around the swimming pool in the front garden of my brother's Christian home. A fairytale venue. Kim's parents put their discontentment aside and attended the wedding. It was a wonderful gesture on their part. They had wanted only the best for their daughter and I fully respected that. In the end, they realised that love conquers all and gave us their blessing. As the years passed, I grew extremely fond of my parents in law and this feeling was reciprocated.

A couple of years after our marriage, we were blessed with our first child. A beautiful baby boy, and we christened him Ryan. A couple of years later our second son, Rory, came along. I was privileged to witness both of my son's natural births. It is the most fantastic and joyous adventure a father can have, a precious gift and an experience that I will cherish for my entire life.

Soon after Rory's birth, a good colleague of mine and I decided to leave the large retailer we worked for and open our own furniture business. Unfortunately, after a period of three years, both the partnership and business failed. That first failure in business served me a lesson and introduced me to a situation that I did not want to return to. I was then approached by an old friend of mine who headed a 'direct-selling' company. I joined as the area manager and within six months was promoted to Regional manager. The work was intense and the hours were very long, spending most weekends away from my young family. The only positive being the earnings. I was making a ton of money, but the company being a 'pyramid type' operation did little to ensure me of it's longevity.

It was at about that period, in the early nineties, that both my brother in laws and I decided to get involved in the liquor industry. We purchased a wine wholesaler and expanded it into a bottling plant. This turned out to be mistake and lesson number two. It was impossible to compete against the giants in the trade and they crushed us. The company was liquidated, but now, having had the experience in the workings of the liquor industry, fate was about to come knocking at my door and it would change the course of my life completely.

**

A very well to do Mauritian born businessman, an old acquaintance of my Dad, approached me to set up a liquor business for him, similar to the one we had owned. He had a dormant liquor license and with his backing and influence with major distillers, I set up a bottling plant and developed new brands. A large portion of the vodka production was exported to a client of his in Eastern Europe.

One weekday morning in early 1994, his secretary called, asking me to come to the head office as he wanted to chat to me urgently. He informed me that he had just returned from a trip abroad and after discussions with a business colleague in Romania, he wanted to move the whole bottling operation there, and would I be interested in moving to Romania.

Romania had at that time began a transition towards democracy and a capital market economy. The 1989 revolution had brought an end to Communist rule and the downfall of its iron-fisted dictator, Nicolae Ceausescu. The country began attracting an increasing amount of foreign investment and after decades of decay, the economy slowly began to transform itself into one of stability.

I was initially sent to Bucharest on a fact finding mission and spent over a week in the capital, looking at prospective factory premises as well as suitable accommodation and viable schools for the boys. I returned to South Africa and stated that if the following conditions were agreed to, I would go. We would be housed at a brand new gated housing development called 'The French Village'. It was situated on the side of a large lake, on the outskirt of the capital. The village had all of the facilities one could wish for and more. We would be lodged in a modern three bed townhouse, with indoor and outdoor pools and tennis courts on our doorstep, as well as a clubhouse with pubs, restaurants and a squash court. Both of my boys would go to a private school, the American School of Bucharest. And of course, I asked for a decent package.

These demands were made in a boardroom full of people and after listening to me, the 'Boss' asked me to come and stand next to him. On enquiring why, he said he wanted to grope me, as he suspected that my balls were made of steel. The whole board room fell apart with laughter. He agreed to all of the demands and within weeks, we shut down the Durban operation, loaded all of the machinery, equipments and raw materials into dozens of containers for shipment to Romania.

Within the first few months of landing in Romania, I had upgraded an old warehouse into a clean and modern bottling plant, employed and trained a working force consisting mainly of ladies and began producing a good quality vodka. We had brought coal to Newcastle!

Kim and I often speak of the time we spent in Bucharest and both agree that it was a great passage in our lives. We met and became friendly with numerous ex-pat families from all over the world, such as Canada, England, Scotland, Australia, Sweden, Israel and many more. We had an incredibly busy social life, always entertaining and being entertained. The boys loved their school, developed an American twang and made friends with classmates from every corner of the planet. To this day, like Kim and I, they have stayed in contact with many of them. While living there, we also visited many European cities. Life was wonderful.

That is until I received a dreadful phone call from South Africa, stating for reasons I was never privy to, that a decision was made and that they were selling their shares to the Romanian partner. I was given the choice of carrying on with the Romanian partner, an individual named Kaufmann, or returning to South Africa. I was not happy with either of these options. From the offset, I never felt comfortable with Kaufmann, a bombastic, mafia-esque type human being who I had no intention of working for. He owned various enterprises in Bucharest and his management style was repulsive to say the least. We butted heads a few times.

The one occasion that sticks out is when he summoned me to his office, which took up half a floor of the Buchuresti Hotel. I had decided that every member of the bottling staff would be rewarded with a bottle of vodka at the end of each week, if targets were met and there were no serious breakages. He took exception to that and in front of all his yes-men at the meeting, ordered me to stop this incentive with immediate effect, as it was costing the company sixty cases of vodka per year. I tried to explain that the staff earned a pittance and that it was proven that this incentive boosted productivity and reduced breakages. He barked at me that his decision was final and the meeting was over, gesturing for me to leave his office.

I was being treated like one of his servants and ordered to go away. I had news for him. It was red mist time. A feeling of deep anger washed over me.

"Do you really think I'm going to just stand here and take this nonsense from you?" I barked back at him. "I have dragged my family halfway around the world to come and help set up this business and do a good job and you speak to me like that? Stuff you, I am not here to take any orders from you." I go on. "The incentive will remain, whether you like it or not."

I noticed beads of sweat developing on his fat forehead, running down and disappearing behind his thick lensed spectacles. He had turned crimson and was furious. How dare anyone stand up to him.

"If you are not happy," I went on, "it's simple. Here are the keys, go run the factory yourself."

With that, I took the bunch of keys from my pocket and placed it on his desk.

You know the saying 'If looks could kill'? Well, if that was real, my ashes would be somewhere in an urn.

After a few seconds of deathly silence which felt like an eternity and with everyone in the room staring at me,

"OK, do it your way." He says, between clenched teeth. "But I warn you, I will be speaking to South Africa about your attitude."

"Do what you want." I replied, picking up the keys and walking out, with all of his henchmen staring at me open mouthed.

**

Having been away from South Africa for a good while and the uncertain future of bringing up our boys there, we decided that as Kim was a British citizen, we would relocate to Great Britain. We were seriously considering that option when we received a phone call from Don and Mark, Kim's brothers. They both resided in Memphis, U.S.A, having secured their green cards via the Irish lottery scheme. They suggested that we join them in the States and while living there, apply for work permits. With all of the contacts I had made in Bucharest, especially within the embassies, I managed to obtain a visa that gave us residency for a period of six months at a time, provided I worked for a Foreign company. This visa had to be continuously renewed.

So, that was that, our minds were made up. We packed our bags, said our goodbyes and within weeks, we were flying over the Atlantic to yet another adventure.

CHAPTER FIVE
FULL CIRCLE

Memphis, Tennessee was going to be our home for the next two and a half years. A vibrant city located on the banks of the Mississippi river, Memphis was famous for introducing the world to the sounds of 'rock and roll' and the 'blues'. It was also home to music legends, such as Elvis Presley, BB king and Johnny Cash. The feeling you get when walking along the world renowned 'Beale Street' in downtown Memphis was everything I ever imagined and more.

We moved into a beautiful, Southern plantation type home on the outskirts of the city, which Don and Mark had purchased prior to our arrival. The boys were placed in a Catholic school, a couple of minutes drive from our home. We immersed ourselves into the American lifestyle and began living the dream. We were rightly informed, everything was bigger and better in the States. No truer words spoken.

My brother in laws and I decide to get involved in the property market - a 'buy to let' scheme. Within the first three months of my arrival, we had purchased a good range of rental properties. By the end of the first year, we possessed a portfolio of forty-seven rental units. As Don and Mark had full time jobs, I was handed the wonderful task of managing, as well as the upkeep, of the properties. I must state upfront, that it turned out to be the most unpleasant and unrewarding job I had ever undertaken.

Our tenants were from a predominantly poor background and most of them turned out to be what was referred to as 'professional renters'. They would pay the deposit, fill in the rental agreement and move in. That would be the last penny you would collect from them. Due to the State property laws, you could not evict them without a court order. That procedure took months and proved to be very costly. Not only would they have stayed in your property for free, they would also abuse the utilities such as gas and electricity which we, as Landlords, were responsible for. To add insult to injury, they would trash the property before vacating. And I am not using the word trash lightly. In many cases, we had to remove human faeces they had plastered on the internal walls, as well as in sinks and bathtubs. It would often take at least a month to clean up and renovate the unit so that it could be rented again. We became 'Slumlords' and that title was very appropriate.

I stuck it out for a couple of years, trying desperately to make this venture work. A fair amount of monies and effort had been invested and failure was not an option. That is, until one bright Saturday afternoon. I had gone to one of our properties to collect overdue rent. I was accompanied by Mark and we were having the usual bad day, collecting more abuse than cash.

On knocking on the door of a second floor flat, I was confronted by a very large African American lady, named Robot. I knew that she was aggressive and could tell immediately that she was either drunk or drugged. On seeing me on her threshold, she went crazy, cursing and spitting in our faces. She slammed the door, telling us to go to hell. It was the final straw. We had been taking abuse all day and I was in no mood to tolerate any more. I stepped back and with all my energy, kicked her door open. I realised immediately that I had made a mistake, and when I saw her rush into the adjoining room, I screamed at Mark, telling him we needed to leg it. I was convinced that she had a gun and would not hesitate using it. I had spent enough time in downtown Memphis and heard enough gunshots to have come to this conclusion. As we reached the bottom of the stairwell, it was not a bullet that missed us, but a heavy steel ladder that came crashing down, missing our skulls by millimetres. We were lucky to get out of there alive.

Many incidents like this one, as well as the fact that getting permanent residence was not going to happen, made us realise that it was irresponsible for us to remain in the States. I had to apply for a Visa renewal every six months and although granted on each occasion, I knew it would be a matter of time until we were told that we had overstayed our welcome. Our boys, now about to enter their secondary school years, needed stability. I was also approaching my mid-forties and we decided that it was now time to settle in the United Kingdom on a permanent basis. It was a bold move but one we had to make. All the properties were put up for sale and on the last day of the year 1998, we left the United States for good. It was also the day our visas expired.

Our stay in America also provided us with an abundance of highlights and good times. We were very close to both of Kim's brothers and their lovely girlfriends, who would later become their wives. We travelled extensively, spending wonderful breaks on the Gulf coast and visited many cities. We made great friends, many of whom we are still in contact with today.

**

Flying over the Atlantic Ocean on our way once again to the unknown and new beginnings, I had many hours to reflect. We were on route to yet another country, with no work prospect, nowhere to live and no idea what our future held. I looked over at my two sons, both sound asleep and always willing and happy to go along with us, wherever we took them. It was now time for me to buckle down and give them stability, a good home and more importantly, a good education. I believed in myself and had complete faith in my abilities. I had no idea how this new chapter in our lives would turn out, but I knew that it was now time to shine. I was determined to make the rest of my life, the best of my life. With these thoughts in mind, our plane touched at London's Heathrow airport in the early hours of New Year's day 1999.

We spent the first week living in a bed and breakfast situated in Paddington Square, Central London. I spent the first couple of days visiting employment agencies, handing in my CV. It did not take me long to realise that London was not the city I wanted to live in. Visiting London as a tourist is totally different to becoming a prospective resident there. The thought of travelling daily on the underground to and from work or school did not sit well with me.

We sent our boys to stay with their grandparents in Wales. They were retired and lived in a quaint village called Cwmbran, situated about half a dozen miles or so from the city of Newport, towards the valleys. We visited them over weekends and I spent most of my time looking around Cardiff and the surrounding areas. It was then that I made the decision to make Wales our home, instead of England. I found the Welsh very friendly, but at the same time extremely colloquial.

We began searching for a place to live and within a week, we moved into a comfortable three bedroom flat in Cyncoed, a pleasant suburb of the Capital city. Our boys were placed in a Catholic school and as per usual, settled well in their new lives. I could now concentrate in finding a job, and started searching for one in earnest.

I came across an advert in the local newspaper that caught my attention. It was a well known window decor company looking at employing a manager for their Newport store, with the added incentive that if all worked out well, you would be invited to purchase the Franchise. I applied for the position with the usual hundreds of others and following a series of ferocious interviews, I was offered the position. No one was more surprised than myself, as I had no experience at all in that field.

The Newport Franchise, I was told, was one of their worst performing stores in a group of over eighty franchises in the UK. After just a week's training at their head office in the Midlands, I took control of the store with Kim as my assistant. She ran the showroom and made appointments, while I went out giving quotes and selling. Within five months of us taking over the franchise, we were now constantly in the top twenty, sales wise. This did not go unnoticed by our Head Office, and we began receiving congratulatory cards, accompanied by bottles of bubbly.

"We need to make an offer now, and buy this Franchise." I told Kim over a weekend. "The more we improve this store, the more money they will want for it."

The following week, the General Manager of the company paid us a visit and I indicated that I was ready to buy the Franchise. He seemed pleased and said he would discuss it with the Directors and would give me an indication of their asking price the following morning. As I suspected, the asking price was now exorbitant and way out of our price range. I was very unhappy and made him aware of my feelings. We improved the business four fold and we were now being penalised for our efforts.

Knowing that he was travelling back North the next morning, I wrote a letter to him with my offer to purchase the franchise for less than half of what they valued it at, reminding him that he was not only getting paid a fair fee for a franchise that was struggling before we began managing it, but he was also getting us in the deal and that was worth a lot. I handed him the letter the moment he walked into the shop the following morning. He immediately opened the envelope and read the contents of the letter. He stood up, extended his hand and simply said,

"You've got a deal, I am happy with the offer. The Franchise is yours, well done."

I was both stunned and excited and in jest shouted at Kim, who was at the back of the store, as she did not want to be present when I handed him the letter,

"Darling, we've offered too much!"

We all had a good laugh and the three of us went out that morning for a celebratory breakfast.

We were now owners of a great little business, which grew from strength to strength. We also began developing and manufacturing our own products and employed a lovely couple from the valleys to help us as sales kept on rising. We were soon in the top ten performing Franchises, and the bottles of Moet and Chandon kept on coming.

***

Within two years of landing in the UK, I became a permanent resident. That allowed us to purchase our first home. We bought a four bedroomed new build on an estate, situated between Newport and Cardiff. We worked hard and lived a good life. The boys were now doing their final grades at St David's college in Cardiff. My niece Mylene and her Husband joined us and managed the Newport shop. This allowed me to open a new franchise in Cardiff. We were now amongst the top performers in the group and instead of bottles of bubbly, we were being rewarded with overseas trips, winning holidays to Florida and many European destinations.

One summer evening, I drove to a holiday park situated to the South of Cardiff, not far from the International airport, to measure and give a quote on a caravan. Parking the car near the caravan, I was overwhelmed by the view that greeted me. Perched on a cliff, it overlooked the mouth of the Severn river which flowed into the English channel. On the opposite side of the river was the English coastline. A spectacular spot. That evening at the dinner table, I describe what I had seen to the family, telling them that it would be an absolute dream to live in that part of the world with its stunning views. Dreams do come true. A year and a half later, we built and moved into a gorgeous five bedroomed home on the edge of the cliff, a stone's throw from the caravan park.

Soon after moving into our new home, I became a British citizen. It was on Monday 20th December 2004 and what a special day that was. Kim and I attended the citizenship ceremony at the Vale of Glamorgan civic offices in the coastal town of Barry. I took the Oath of Allegiance to Her Majesty The Queen and a pledge of loyalty to the United Kingdom. After singing 'God bless the Queen' in full voice, hand on heart, we ended the day with other recipients and their families, having numerous cocktails in the Mayor's parlour.

The next eight years of our lives were blissful. We lived in a picturesque little Welsh village, surrounded by kind and pleasant neighbours. The Welsh people I met over the years, and that's hundreds of them given the nature of my work, were arguably the kindest people on the planet. There is a saying that every Welsh person is born with 'music in their heart and poetry in their soul'. Too true.

The boys prospered, excelling in their school exams and both going on to University. Again, both performed extremely well, obtaining good degrees from The University of Glamorgan. Ryan, obtaining a first, went on to complete his Masters. Giving them both a good education was paramount to us. But more than wanting them to be well-educated, we wanted them above all to mature into good, responsible and caring young men. They achieved all of that and more. Having done and accomplished many things so far in my own life, nothing compares to the wonderful moments I've experienced as a father. I could not have wished for better sons and I will keep on hugging them and telling them how proud I am of them until my final breath.

Before moving on, I feel that I need to talk of my excessive devotion to my beloved Chelsea Football Club. My family and friends see me as an extreme fanatic, and I have no case to argue against that. Both Rory, also a devout supporter, and I, had the good fortune of watching them play at the Bridge on many occasions. What a great day out that was, starting at the crack of dawn, we would train down to London, enjoy a couple of pints at the 'Slug and Lettuce' and join fellow supporters with chants, before making our way to the stadium.

A day that will be embedded in my mind forever, was the Carling Cup final of 2005. We were playing against arch rivals, Liverpool, at the Millennium Stadium. My good friend Anthony, also a Chelsea die-hard fan, had managed to secure two perfectly positioned seats, halfway up and middle of grandstand.

The game was minutes from kick off and we were baffled that a complete row of seats in front of us remained unoccupied. Eventually a young and frail looking Japanese couple, each with a fancy camera dangling from straps around their necks, made their way up and took their seats at the end of the still empty row. They were obviously tourists and seemed in awe at what was going on around them. The deafening chants, the wild cursing, the raw abuse and flag waving. Both of their cameras were soon in action, capturing images of the dramatic scenes that unfolded before them.

It was during the singing of the anthem that Anthony and I first spot 'them' making their way up the steps towards the empty seats. At least thirty of them, all shaved heads, all heavily tattooed, all dressed in leather and heavy boots. They took their seats in front of us, and it is clear that they had spent the previous couple of hours ravaging the stock of a nearby pub. We also knew that they would not hesitate to demonstrate their zeal with obsessive enthusiasm if the occasion to do so arose.

The occasion did arise, in the 80th minute of the game to be precise. Chelsea was trailing by a goal. A free kick glanced off Steven Gerrard's head and floated over their keeper's outstretched hands, into the back of their net. An own goal. A double whammy in fact. The stadium erupts. As per customary, Anthony and I hug and jump up and down to the beat of huge cheers. The stadium shakes with pure euphoria. We notice that all the shaved heads also celebrate in a massive group hug. And then it happened, almost in slow motion. Under their enormous weight, the pyramid of bodies began collapsing. Like an avalanche, they descended on top of the poor Japanese couple, who had remained seated, watching the mayhem develop around them with pure fear in their eyes. Within seconds, they had disappeared from sight, lying helpless under a mountain of flesh.

Fearing they could suffocate, Anthony and I tried to pull the bodies off them. They were not budging. Fortunately, the incident must have been spotted on CCTV, and within minutes we were surrounded by an army of stewards, who pull the shaved heads off, one by one, revealing the poor, petrified couple, laying flat on their backs at the bottom of the pile.

Once freed, and looking shocked, ruffled and bewildered, they both disappeared in haste, never to be seen again. The shaved heads, totally unfazed, carried on with their wild celebrations, as if nothing happened. This is what English football is all about, after every single game, there is always a good story to tell. Oh, for the record, the mighty Blues claim the trophy, 3-2 in extra time. Anthony and I leave the stadium, and head to the nearest pub, arm in arm, chanting and deliriously happy.

***

It was during the early winter months of 2011 that Kim and I took a decision that would totally alter the course of our lives. The boys, after graduating, had left the nest. Rory was first to go. He decided to take a year out and go travelling, visiting Australia, New Zealand and Japan. On his return, he began work with a web design company located in Bristol, and moved to the English City. He still works there to this day.

Ryan, after completing his masters, began work for an international IT company. He moved to a flat in Cardiff Bay, but he indicated that he also wanted to take a year out for travels, to China and Australia.

Both of our sons lives were being filled with new experiences. Kim and I were left on our own, living in a much too big a house for just the two of us. I suggested that we should also fill our lives with fresh experiences. After having holidayed in Mauritius in 2008, I had this niggling feeling of going back to the Island to live there for a few years. I was now sixty years old, much too early to retire, but if we sold our home and business it would provide enough funds for our next adventure. The years were now rushing by and I believed in the principle that I would be more disappointed by the risks I did not take and things we did not do, than by the ones we did do. I needed a fresh challenge.

On top of that, we had also just lost our beloved Phoebe, a beautiful Cavalier King Charles, that had been part of our lives for eight years, before developing and succumbing to a heart murmur. She had been our constant companion, and was cherished as an important member of our family. Her passing had a profound effect on all of us, and left a huge void in our lives. The house became an emptier place without her. We had been living in the UK for over fourteen years now, the boys had begun their own lives, it was time for new adventures.

The only hiccup was that our timing was way out, economically. We were in the middle of a global economic downturn and it was definitely not the right time to sell properties and businesses. After much deliberation, we decided to still go for it. Our minds were made up, and we had the full backing of the boys. During the early months of 2012, we sold everything we worked so hard for, well below market value, with no ill-feelings or regrets. We were excited at what laid ahead of us, we loaded the container and flew out at the end of January, destination Mauritius. I had left the island over fifty years ago, and here I was, going back 'home' - I had come full circle.

CHAPTER SIX
IMAGES, COCKTAILS AND AFRICA

Over a century ago, on setting foot in Mauritius, Mark Twain famously quoted: 'Mauritius was made first, and then Heaven, and that Heaven was copied after Mauritius'. Some things never change.

After an overnight flight and with the rising sun, we approached Mauritius from the West. We broke through the clouds and there below us laid the Island in all of its glory. Ringed by coral reefs, snow white sand and azure lagoons, we approached the airport from the East coast, flying over the Le Morne mountains. Palm trees, tropical plants and rows and rows of emerald sugar cane plantations, greeted our descent and landing.

We spent our first week in a gorgeous hotel on the East coast, witnessing breathtaking sunsets every evening. A day after our arrival, we spent the day in the capital, Port Louis, where I managed to update my birth certificate, and with that I applied for an identity card which was granted within a couple of hours. For a small island, they were well organised.

Armed with an ID card, I opened a bank account and we began our search for a house to rent. This did not take long either. we knew where we wanted to live on the island and after viewing a couple of homes in the Black River area, our charming and efficient estate agent showed us a home, located on the upside of the Le Morne mountain. It looked out over a manicured golf course, onto a turquoise bay with a small islet in the middle of it. It was paradise and the house was ultra comfortable, with the added bonus of a sparkling pool. We moved in within a week. Our Island adventure had begun and we were both ecstatic.

The efficiency of the Mauritian people and companies kept impressing me. Within a couple of days of settling in, we had a telephone landline, wifi and cable TV. Our container arrived a week later, we employed a maid named Marlene and I revelled talking to her in Creole and finding out in detail about our surrounding area. Our first months on the Island were pure bliss. Mornings were taken with long walks up the side of the mountains, taking long pauses to admire the amazing scenery that stretched out below us. In the afternoon, we would go down to the beach to have lunch under the filao trees, the Mauritian version of the casuarina. We would swim and snorkel in the warm lagoons and ended the days with a couple of cold lagers, watching a spectacular sunset.

The evenings were spent with me experimenting on dishes, from a recipe which Marlene had given me in the morning. We dined on the verandah, and often, just the two of us, danced the night away under the inquisitive look of our adopted cat.

We purchased a car and spent many days exploring the Island. We wanted to go back to Church and again Marlene suggested we come to hers, a small Chapel situated on the water's edge, on the other side of the Morne mountain. We thoroughly enjoyed the Sunday Masses, surrounded by the Locals, singing joyful hymns in creole, accompanied by banjos and the beating of tambourines.

During that period, we had frequent visitors. My sisters Micheline and Marielle stayed with us as well as Josee and her daughter Francoise. Over the Christmas period, we had Rory visiting us and he was followed by my niece Mylene and her family. She is the one that worked with us in the UK, but had returned to live permanently in South Africa. We also met up on a couple of occasions with my good friend Michel, who was married to one of my cousins. He too was involved with the Durban company which had sent me to Romania, where he had visited us frequently. We had developed a very close friendship. Most of his brothers and sisters had remained in Mauritius and he visited them regularly. Our friend Mandie from Dubai also visited. She loved the Island so much, she came twice. It was during one of those visits that I noticed that my sister, Micheline, was behaving strangely. Not long afterwards, she was sadly diagnosed with Pick's disease, an aggressive form of dementia.

Although being kept pretty busy, I soon realised that 'retirement' was not for me. Also, we did not have sufficient funds to carry on enjoying the outrageous lifestyle we were getting used to. I had a great, relaxing six months, but was now becoming agitated. I needed to do something. I wanted to start a business aimed at the tourist market and it had to be in the North of the Island. The South East, where we lived, apart from a couple of high class hotels, was well off the beaten track. The ideal location would be in or near the seaside village of Grand Baie, which was always packed with tourists. I knew full well however that finding premises there would be virtually impossible and if something did become available, the rent would be astronomical.

It was during one of our outings there, after lunching on the beach and walking back to the carpark, that Kim noticed a small notice stuck on the window of a little corner store. The notice, written in French, indicated that they had space to let, suitable for a small retail unit. I made a note of the name of the person to speak to and the contact number. That same evening I called a lady by the name of Artee. She explained to me that they wanted to let the space next to their shop and they were currently using it as storage for their empties. It had shutter doors that opened onto the main street, the busiest street in

Grand Baie. Bingo. I could hardly contain my excitement. I made an appointment to meet with her the following morning to view the premises.

The distance between where we lived to Grand Baie, on the other side of the Island, was roughly an hour and a half journey by car, depending on the traffic.

We met with Artee and her husband Rajesh. They were to become good friends of ours and to this day we still communicate with them. Their family owned the large property which lined the street corner to corner. An imposing three storey building with retail shops, a pharmacy and a restaurant at the bottom and rental apartments on the upper levels. The premises in question, was a dingy, dark storeroom, sandwiched between the pharmacy and their store. It was perfect.

A lot of work had to be done to convert it into a retail unit and I already had in mind what to do with it. Within an hour, we had agreed on the terms and a lease was drawn up and signed. We had now embarked on a new business venture, located, arguably, in the best trading spot Mauritius had to offer.

I employed a carpenter and together, within a month, we transformed an ugly storeroom into a gem of a shop, opening out onto the main road. During that period I applied for a business license, which was granted, and we named our little business 'Images'. It was a printing shop where one could print their holiday pictures. We also took and printed passport photos and filled the little shop to the brim with local souvenirs, postcards, baskets, underwater cameras and a lot more paraphernalias. We employed a young lady, known to the Landlady, to run the store and Images opened for business. The little shop was a success from day one.

The only downside was that we lived on the other side of the Island and having to drive North three times per week was becoming tiresome. We replenished our stock weekly, spending the day in Port Louis, visiting various Chinese wholesalers. This alone was quite an experience. Our main supplier being a small shop located on the corner of two busy streets in Port Louis. The moment you entered the premises, an energetic sales assistant tagged on to you for the duration of your visit. The shop was always jam packed with buyers, mainly street and beach vendors replenishing their stock. Every inch of the wall and ceiling space was plastered with merchandise - thousands of items.

We squeezed our way around the showroom making our selections. A dozen miniature pirogues, two dozen tortoise shells dodos, and so on. All Mauritian souvenirs, and all made in China. Once we had selected all of the required items, we followed our assistant who handed our order to the 'Boss' - a Billy Bunter lookalike Chinese man, who was sat behind a small desk with a large abacus placed in front of him. He looked up and his face broke out into a huge grin when he saw me.

"Bonjour Monsieur Image!" He shouted out. "Back so soon? Business must be good in Grand Baie."

Looking at the list, his fingers went to work on the abacus, dividing and adding a variety of beans on a counting frame at a furious pace. At the same time he informed me that they only had six of a special cap in stock, so I would be six short. Within seconds he gave me the total amount owing, minus the now customary little discount that went with it. There was no need to check, he was always spot on. I handed over a wad of Rupees that also got counted at record pace before disappearing into a deep drawer next to him, bursting with cash. He shouted out an order in chinese and a wooden peg dangling at the end of a string was dropped in front of him, from a hole in the ceiling. He attached the order, and the peg was pulled up and disappeared into the hole in the attic - the storeroom.

"Bonne journee, Monsieur Images. Your order will be ready in five minutes." He said as he waved me goodbye.

We made our way to the exit and waited outside on the pavement. Like clockwork, we heard the shout "Images order ready, coming down," as a large box containing all of our purchases was lowered from a bigger hole in the ceiling. Shopping done. No fuss, no computers, no waiting, just great speed and service at it's 'Made in China' best.

***

During Rory's visit in December, we received word from Ryan, that he wanted to visit us in Mauritius in mid January, on his way back home. He had spent a year in China and Australia and he would spend a couple of weeks with us on the Island. It was at about the same time that I was approached by Neel, the Landlord's brother, enquiring if I was interested in leasing the restaurant. The current Lessor, a Frenchman, had an extension to his work permit declined and had to leave the Island.

I called Ryan in Australia, telling him about this opportunity and would he be interested at getting involved in this venture with me. He would need to extend his stay in Mauritius to help me as I wanted to make extensive changes and also rebrand the restaurant completely. He agreed and within a couple of days, I signed a new lease, paid the Frenchman a goodwill fee and presto, we were now new owners of a restaurant, a couple of meters away from the Images boutique.

Ryan landed in Mauritius mid-January, and we got to work immediately. First stop, the Government offices in Port Louis. Within a couple of hours, we emerged with his Mauritian ID card and permanent residence on the Island if he so wished. As our lease on our house was coming to an end, we decided to move to the North of the Island to be closer to the businesses. We found a very nice bungalow with pool and gorgeous entertainment area. We moved in at the beginning of February.

With the help of the same carpenter, we transformed the look of the restaurant completely. It would offer mainly Mauritian food, with a bar for patrons to enjoy exotic cocktails. We named it 'Lazy Dodo' and opened for business in March. Again, it did well from the very beginning. We now had two good little businesses on this idyllic Island. I woke up everyday, knowing the sun would shine and the birds would sing endlessly. I went to work in my usual uniform of shorts, T-shirts and flip flops.

The months passed by lazily and it was towards the end of June that Ryan announced that he wanted to get back to the UK and resume his career in the world of technology. He felt that Island life was not for him in the long term, and he now needed a place to settle down and make his home, and that place was Bristol where Rory lived. He flew from the Island at the end of June. Having spent the past six months working closely with him and having his company in the evenings, his departure left us both in a void. A very sad one.

During the months that followed, we kept on receiving visitors. My sister Micheline visited on a couple of occasions and we noticed that her condition was deteriorating at an alarming rate. Rory visited us again over the festive season and it was the day that we dropped him off at the airport that we both realised that there was no need in fooling ourselves any longer. We could not live away from our boys on a permanent basis. The thought of not having their presence in our lives regularly was not what we wanted.

Island life, although very pleasing, was also becoming a desperately lonely spot for Kim and I. Apart from the people we were involved with at work, we did not meet and make many friends. The family I had on the island, a couple of cousins, kept pretty much to themselves. Then again, we did not make too much of an effort to mix with them as well.

The one thing that still peeved me in Mauritius, was the continuous existence of what we used to call 'Les Grand Blancs'. On leaving Mauritius so many years ago, I really believed that they were an endangered species and had hoped that they would suffer the same fate as the poor Dodo bird and become extinct. I was wrong. They are still alive and well, and go about their business with the continuous misinterpreted perception that the whole Island belongs to them. To define a 'Grand Blanc' in the kindness possible way, is to describe them as a group of wealthy white families who, by virtue of their bank balances and land ownership, see themselves in a completely different bracket to us normal mortals. With their air of superiority and grandeur comes arrogance and a good dose of nastiness. They live in their own 'camps', residing in large villas attached to 'their' own private beach and sea, which no one dare trespass. They frequent yacht clubs where only they have the right of membership. They have perfectly located private suites at the 'Champ de Mars' racecourse and the eccentricity goes on.

The strangeness of things however, is that once you remove them from their habitat, even with their fancy surnames and billions of Rupees, they become normal human beings again. I met many 'Grand Blancs' on my travels outside of Mauritius. I even met one in a pub in Bucharest of all places. We spent a great evening together, having drinks and sharing jokes in Creole. Sadly, this would not have happened in Mauritius, where they only move in their own sacred circle. Enough said on this matter.

All of the above made us realise that we wanted to get back 'home' to our boys. Even the magical life we had made for ourselves in Mauritius was not enough to keep us away from them. We knew that this would be our final venture and we decided that we should spend a few years in Durban, to spend time with my siblings and be near Micheline, before going back to the UK for good. We had become professional packers, so a container was ordered and loaded. Again, businesses were sold and sad farewells exchanged. We were on our way to Africa.

***

After a pleasant four hour flight over the Indian Ocean, we landed at Durban International airport. It was nearing the end of March. After staying at my sister Marielle's home for a couple of weeks, we moved into a charming simplex within a gated community, North of Durban. It was good to be back on

South African soil, albeit a very different country to the one we had left twenty years ago.

After two decades of democracy, beautiful South Africa was now being totally mismanaged by a corrupt government. Allegedly, rampant corruption was the order of the day. Economic inequality still persisted and the huge increase in crime and violence impacted everyone's lives. In suburban areas like where we lived, most of the inhabitants lived in homes that had high walls, electric fences, alarm systems and CCTV. This was the norm, unfortunately. Even driving around, one needed to always be alert, given the high rise of car hijacking in the country.

According to the locals, the above doom and gloom was far outweighed by the good and positive. The weather, beautiful landscapes and beaches makes South Africa one of the most enchanting countries in the world and provides them with a great lifestyle. Whilst living there again for a short while, my feeling was that its democracy was taking a turn for the interesting. A fairly new political party, the Democratic Alliance, led by an intelligent liberal young man, was making steady progress and gaining support across the racial divide. The ruling party, the ANC, was at long last beginning to lose its dominance due mainly to accusations of multiple scandals and corruption. I am by no means a Politician and certainly in no position to offer a solution, except to say that I really hope that the good will eventually outweigh the bad and the 'Rainbow' nation will one day become this fascinating, corrupt free country it deserves to be. After all, it is the only country in the world that has produced two Nobel Peace Prize winners that lived in the same street, Vilakazi street, Soweto.

After having to go back to Mauritius for a month to sort out business matters, I returned to Durban and immediately started thinking of what to do next. I was not going to spend months doing nothing, as what happened in Mauritius. Being idle is definitely not a part of my DNA.

I decided that since my brother, Christian, was still involved in the furniture industry, I should set up a small manufacturing unit and produce good and affordable, quality furniture. His help and experience would be invaluable in placing the products into retail outlets. My good friend, Michel, joined me in this new venture and it was a perfect partnership. Being an accountant, he would take care of all of the administrative side of the business and let me concentrate on the manufacturing and marketing side. We found a suitable commercial unit in a good location, purchased the machinery, employed a small work force and began trading towards the end of 2014. As it was something I had never done before, the first couple of months proved fairly challenging. It was also physically demanding. But as the months passed and our products came to life, I began enjoying it, especially as we slowly but surely began making inroads in the marketplace. We were approached by two lovely ladies who contracted us to manufacture mirrors for them. We agreed and added that to our growing list of products.

Suddenly, I found myself caught up in a whirlwind of activities which started at 6.00am on a Monday morning and lasted, non-stop, until 4.00pm on a Friday afternoon. I often had to work evenings and weekends to get units out to very demanding customers. Is this really what I had come back to South Africa for? Not really. We came back to spend as much quality time as we possibly could with my family. I was not achieving that. However, I did meet up with my brother, Christian, on numerous Friday afternoons after work at a pub, a stone's throw from where we lived. I cherished the couple of hours we spent together, having a laugh and reminiscing about the good old days and past experiences.

Over weekends, we spent as much time as we could with Marielle, her husband Roger, who was more a brother to me than an in-law, and their families. I tried to see Micheline as often as I could, but that became increasingly difficult, given her medical condition. My sincere regret is that I did not get to spend enough quality time with the rest of my other siblings. I did, however, manage to have all nine brothers and sisters for a wonderful get together and dinner at our place a few months before I fell ill. Planning this reunion was no easy task, for geographic and other reasons, but we did get together and it was a wonderful gathering that lasted long into the night. At one stage, our eldest sister, Josee, had us all gathered in a circle, that same circle of strength, and spoke emotionally of how we had all lived our lives beautifully and raised our children, with many of us overcoming difficult obstacles along the way. She credited it all to the way we were brought up, our closeness, our faith and the tenacity we had all inherited from our Father. I often look at a photo taken that evening, of the nine of us with our spouses and wonder if we'll ever all be together again. I sincerely hope so.

It was approximately eighteen months after arriving in South Africa, that I began feeling unusually tired. I would get home every evening feeling exhausted. I remember clearly, on visits to the shopping mall, asking Kim to walk at a slower pace as my legs felt like 'jelly' and I struggled to keep up with her. We joked about it, putting it down to me getting old. During the month of December, I had a long chat with my business partner, Michel, indicating to him that the running of the factory was getting me down. I lacked the energy and suggested we sold it. It had started doing well and we would be able to easily recuperate our investment. He agreed wholeheartedly and we decided to put the business up for sale in the new year.

In January 2016, I started having terrible back pains and felt permanently fatigued. I met with a couple of Commercial agents and they assured me that, at the right price, we should have no problem in finding a buyer for our small business. It was during mid-January, that I received an early morning phone call from one of the agents, saying he had two prospective buyers lined up. He was bringing one to view the business that same morning and the other towards the end of the week. Michel was with me when the call came through and we were both excited at the prospect that we may have the business sold pretty soon. Within half an hour or so of him leaving me, he called asking me to put everything on hold as his eldest son was interested in the business. A short while later, he returned with his son, who decided there and then that he would buy me out and that they already had someone in mind to run the factory. A deal was agreed on and I was very pleased that Michel and Son were now the new proprietors.

Whilst all of this was taking place, I had met up again, by pure chance, with an old Italian friend of mine, who now lived in Johannesburg. Piero, having been involved in the tannery side of the leather industry his whole working life, had sold all of his tanneries and gone into imports and wholesale of Leather. He was doing very well in the Transvaal and suggested I join him and represent the brand in KwaZulu Natal. It would be a lot easier for me, work wise, without the constant pressure of managing a workforce and meeting tight deadlines on a daily basis. With the Leather, I could work at my own pace. After visiting the Johannesburg operation in February, I set up a small showroom in Durban and began trading in March.

In the meantime, the back pains worsened. I visited the doctor on a couple of occasions and it all pointed to the sciatica nerves. I was prescribed stronger painkillers and more anti-inflammatories, the effect of which only lasted short term. The weeks turned into months and the pain persisted. Walking and just standing upright becoming a struggle. Unknown to me, all the while, a cancerous tumor was growing inside of me, going up the base of my spine.

That all led up to that fateful day when I had my blood tested, and the results revealing the severity of my condition. That day changed my life forever. I was now no longer in control of my destiny.

CHAPTER SEVEN
GOOSEBUMPS

It was Saturday 6th August 2016. I had broken the bad news to both of my sons the previous evening. I spent a sleepless night, lying on my back, knowing that they would be hurting. Kim had gone into town to collect my air ticket and organise a travel cash card. I was booked to fly out to the UK the following Tuesday, five days after being diagnosed.

As per usual, despite the non-stop consumption of painkillers, my back pain persisted and I spent the morning propped in bed, answering phone calls from well wishers. A call came through from Ryan and Rory. They had met to discuss the week ahead and assured me that everything would be organised and ready for my arrival. I would stay at Ryan's flat and have his bedroom and he would sleep on the sleeper couch in the lounge. They wanted a list from me of food I would enjoy and more importantly had made an appointment for me at the local surgery.

Whatever your condition, the system insisted that you had to go through a doctor, who, after examination, would refer you to a Specialist. I already had my National Health Services number and that as well as the address of my previous GP in the UK was given to them, so that they could access my medical records prior to my arrival.

I kept the conversation very lighthearted with both of them and although I could sense their anxiety about my condition, I could also detect their excitement at both their Mom and I returning to the UK. After a fair amount of banter and reassurance from me that, with them by my side, I was more than ready to fight this disease, we hung up. I had also informed them that my daughter, Chantal, was visiting me that afternoon and I was very excited at seeing her again.

Being excited at seeing Chantal after a separation of more than twenty years was a gross understatement. The last time we had spent time with her was a couple of years before we left South Africa. This is a complex matter and not one I would like to relive or write about. It was a dark and painful period in my life and fortunately, I had the support of my family and then Kim, to help me get through it. Sadly, this resulted in me missing out on a huge period of her life and I was not around to see her blossom into the beautiful woman she is today.

One evening, out of the blue, a few months after arriving in Durban, I received a phone call from Chantal. We had a short conversation and on hanging up I told Kim that it was a strange call that left me baffled and a little upset. She still referred to me as 'Gilbert' and wanted to know about the legalities of getting a work permit in the UK. I gave her as much information as I could on the matter. It felt more like a business call and not the type I would have expected, even though we both made some vague promise to remain in touch from now on.

It was now virtually a year later, on the very same day that I had given blood samples, that I received another call from her. It was a Tuesday evening, sitting propped up in the lounge, Kim brought the phone to me, mouthing silently that it was Chantal.

"Hello Dad," she said in the softest voice. "How are you?"

I was stunned. The last time she called me 'Dad' was over thirty years ago, when she was still a toddler.

"I'm fine." I reply, my voice trembling a little.

"Actually, I lie." I went on. "I have been having terrible back pains for the past six months and had my blood taken for tests."

"Probably just pinched nerves and high cholesterol, nothing serious." I reassure her. "Anyway, I will be getting the results on Thursday and I'll let you know."

"I'm very sad to hear that," She replies. "If you don't mind, I will call you on Thursday evening to find out about the results."

With that, we go on to have the most beautiful conversation. Her, enquiring about Kim and the boys, and me finding out what she has been up to for the past twenty years. As we were about to hang up, she utters a couple of words that will stay with me forever.

"Dad," She says gently. "Before I go, I just want you to know that I love you, and have always loved you."

When Kim walks back in the room, it takes me several minutes to compose myself. With a huge lump in my throat, I tell her what had just happened. I have my daughter back.

Thursday soon arrived, along with the dreadful news. That evening, as promised, Chantal called to enquire about the results. I give her the bad news and to my astonishment, she reacts as if she already knew.

"I had a feeling you were seriously ill." She said. "I will be coming up to Durban to see you within the next couple of weeks."

At that stage, I had absolutely no idea that I would be flying out to the UK the following Tuesday, but told her of my plans of getting back home for immediate treatment. She said she would call me the following day to find out if I had managed to get on a flight and for when.

We hung up and this time I was completely bewildered. How did she know about my illness? She lived thousands of kilometers away in Cape Town. There was no way that the diagnosis, which I had only found out about myself a couple of hours earlier, could have reached her. Most of my siblings and family that lived in the same city were still unaware of my condition.

The following day, Friday, we had dozens of visitors during the course of the morning and afternoon. Kim had managed to get me on an outbound flight, leaving the following Tuesday afternoon. It was just past midday when Chantal called again. With our lounge abuzz with visitors, I took the call in the bedroom.

"Hello Chantal," I said, sounding as upbeat as I could. "We've managed to get a flight to London this Tuesday coming. I am so sorry it's so soon and I will not be able to see you before I leave."

"Not to worry, Dad." She replied. "I'm calling to let you know that I've just landed in Durban. I am calling from the airport."

"You've just flown in from Cape Town?" I replied, dumbfounded.

"Yes, I did not want to risk not seeing you before you leave." She goes on, "if it's okay with you, I'd like to see you tomorrow afternoon, as I fly back for work the next day."

I was speechless for a long while.

"Of course it is okay with us, it's been too long since we've seen you, so much to catch up with."

"Thank you so much for coming all that way to see me." I stuttered back.

With that, we hang up. I go back to the lounge and tell Kim and my visiting siblings that Chantal had just landed in Durban to meet with me. We were all mystified.

Saturday afternoon soon arrives and I was delighted that I would soon be reunited with her, but also a little apprehensive.

I felt uneasy, having been an unavailable Father for so many years which deprived both of us from a healthy and loving Father-Daughter relation. I knew that the best way forward was to allow this relationship to move at an appropriate, natural pace, without forcing anything from either party. I was comfortable in the knowledge that I was the innocent victim of this alienation but not being present in her life for such a long period of time was still terribly painful.

Kim met her at the door when she arrived and after a long hug, showed her the way to the bedroom, where I was propped up in bed. She had not changed one bit. Her long dark hair, her beautiful smiling eyes and velvet soft skin, the kindness in her voice. It was exactly how I remembered her. We hugged for a long while, my eyes filled with tears. Happy tears. We spoke at length about our lives, her telling me about her education, work experiences and the relationships she had. I, in turn, told her of our adventures and brought her up to date with her brothers accomplishments and their whereabouts.

It was a wonderful and positive reunion. We both ignored the past and focused instead on the future. With my deteriorating health and not knowing what laid ahead, I had no intention of dwelling on the lost years. I now had to make the most of the present and the days ahead.

During our conversation that afternoon, I asked her how she came to know about my poor health and that, frankly, both

Kim and I were flabbergasted at the turn of events. This is what she had to say:

Over many years, she had always felt my presence in her life. I was always by her side. A couple of weeks before contacting me, she no longer felt my presence near her and it disturbed her a great deal. This feeling lasted and it began worrying her to the extent that she confided in a close friend, who suggested she should have a sitting with a lady she had heard of, who did readings. Apparently she was very good and immensely popular. Chantal visited her on the Tuesday morning, the very same day I had my blood taken for analysis. After chatting to her for a while, the lady told her to make contact with me as soon as possible as I was seriously ill, suggesting she should call me that same evening.

Both Kim, sitting on the edge of the bed, and I, stared at her open mouthed and covered in goosebumps. I have always been very skeptic of clairvoyants and psychics, or any person for that matter, who claimed to have a supernatural power to perceive events in the future. What we had just heard was mind-blowing. Could this be an amazingly accurate reading from a gifted psychic, or someone lucky enough to have faked the truth. Either way, I did not care. All I knew was that it had brought Chantal back into our lives, and for that I will be forever grateful to this lady.

The rest of the afternoon was spent chatting, laughing and simply appreciating each other's company. She told me that she had met a Scot named Scott, who lived in Edinburgh and she often visited him and her sister who had moved to London. Her next visit, she hoped, would be over the festive season and we agreed that it would be the perfect time for her to be reunited with her two brothers. After spending a good couple of hours with us, she left, promising to call in again the next day before flying back to Cape Town. The time we spent with her turned out to be a wonderfully positive and loving experience.

The next couple of days went by quickly. We had streams of visitors, with brothers, sisters, nephews, nieces, cousins and friends coming to say goodbye and wish me well. The atmosphere was always jovial and positive. All of the words of encouragement, laughter and never ending hugs comforted me over the days leading up to my departure. How fortunate am I, to have family and friends that will prove so difficult to say goodbye to. I kept reminding myself that I was going away to receive the best care possible and that I would soon be back on vacation, feeling my good old self again.

Tuesday arrived and the car journey to the airport was a silent affair. All of the goodbyes had been said and accompanying me to the airport was my sister Marielle, her husband Roger, my brother Henri and Kim. Checking in was a breeze. Flying first class meant red carpet treatment all the way. Final sad goodbyes and hugs were said and shared. I walked through custom control and entered the departure lounge. I knew it would not be long now before I heard the clicking sound of seat belts around me and the announcement from the cockpit indicating that we were ready for take off. I was on my way.

CHAPTER EIGHT
A LONG FORTNIGHT

They say that every individual's first experience of something is usually the best. This was no exception. Flying first class for the first time was indeed quite an experience. The VIP treatment you receive from the moment you board the plane is truly amazing.

Unfortunately, prior to that, I had been let down badly at the Johannesburg airport, having landed there for my connecting flight. As the domestic and international terminals were miles apart, Kim had organised for wheelchair assistance, as there is no way I could have walked that distance with my bad back. On landing, I informed the flight steward of my predicament and he assured me that once I left the aircraft, there would be someone waiting for me on the other side of the exit tunnel to assist me. However, when I arrived, nobody was waiting.

I enquired with every airport staff member who walked past me and nobody showed any bother, except telling me that an attendant would be with me shortly. Nobody came. The minutes ticked by and I had a connecting flight to catch. I then made the wrong and painful decision to walk to the departure terminal. By the time I reached the boarding gate, I had a torturous pain in my lower back, running up my spine. I was soaked, sweating cold. I swallowed a bunch more painkillers and shuffled into the plane.

I was shown to my seat by the flight attendant, who immediately noticed that I was not well. I was pale, sweaty and shaking with pain. She enquired whether I felt capable of flying such a long distance. The last thing I needed now was to be taken off of the flight for health reasons. I lied, saying that I suffered from sciatica and that I was not assisted as per our request and had had to walk a long distance, which worsened my condition. I assured her that I had taken medication and would be fine shortly. She relaxed, assuring me that she would investigate why I was not helped and would make sure I got proper assistance when we landed at Heathrow. I thanked her.

My mobile rang and it was Kim. I told her about my bad experience, but all was now well and we were about to take off. She confirmed that Rory would be at the airport waiting for me and wished me a safe trip. Minutes later, the plane was hurtling down the runway for takeoff.

Sadly, with a sore back, it was not possible to fully appreciate the comfort and impeccable service I was experiencing in first class. For dinner, after handing you a menu, they convert the area around you into a mini dining area, complete with white tablecloth, silver cutlery, fine china and even fresh flowers in a small vase. The plating of the food and attention to detail made you feel you were eating in a five star restaurant. After dinner and suffering through half of 'The Jungle Book', I felt that it was time to get some sleep. The flight attendant proceeded to convert my seat into a flat, comfortable bed, with linen sheets, pillows and a blanket. As I laid on my back, staring up at the ceiling, I began to feel excited. Soon, I would be reunited with my boys.

After a couple of hours of good sleep and an equally good breakfast, we touched down at Heathrow, on time. I prayed for a window of pain free time. I wanted to enjoy meeting up with Rory and to feel okay for the long drive to Bristol. My prayers were answered, I only had a dull ache. The kind flight attendant did not let me down, I was assisted all the way from the moment I stepped off the plane, through border control and onto baggage collection.

As I made my way through the sliding doors, into the arrivals lounge, I spotted Rory immediately. He stood there with an anxious look on his face. He had expected me to come through in a wheelchair. He spotted me and his face broke into a wonderful, welcoming smile. We hugged for a while and he said he was surprised at how well I looked. I told him about the joy of flying first class, as we made our way to the carpark, where his girlfriend Elinor was waiting for us. I knew her well, as she and Rory had started dating about a year before we left Cardiff.

Car loaded, we crawled our way out of the airport traffic and onto the M4, a highway I've travelled down many times. We headed west and an hour and a half later, we entered the city of Bristol.

Recently, Bristol was given 'the best city to live in Britain' award. Famous for its art, culture and numerous festivals, it is packed into an area easily explored by foot or on a bike, offering all of the excitement of a big city. It also boasts the largest cluster of computer design and manufacturing companies outside of Silicon Valley. A perfect location for both of my sons to pursue their careers. Bristol has been their home for over five years now.

Having fought our way through the traffic of the city centre, we arrive at Ryan's flat. It is located about a mile away from the centre, within a green suburb and a pleasant walking distance from Temple Meads station, from where you can connect to all major cities in the UK. His flat, a neat bachelor pad, was of good proportion and nicely furnished. A massive flat TV screen takes centre stage in his lounge and connected to it are all sorts of gaming gadgets. His bedroom also doubles up as his study, complete with desk, computer and a space age type chair. The flat was on ground level, with its own enclosed garden. Looking around, I knew we would be comfortable living with him until we found somewhere suitable to move into.

After a good lunch prepared by Rory and Elinor, I decide to take a nap. It had been a long day and I was pleased my back was holding up. I wake up to voices coming from the lounge. I immediately recognise Ryan's voice. He had just got home from work. I call out to him. He comes in, jumps in bed and gives me a long hug. Rory joins in and the three of us lay in bed for the next hour or so, catching up and discussing the days ahead. Elinor had gone out to get some groceries and would be back later to collect Rory.

They inform me that they had taken every other day off work, so that one of them will be with me all of the time, until Kim would arrive in a couple of weeks. I tried to talk them out of it, realising it would be coming out of their holiday allowance, but they were not budging. After dinner, we chatted long into the night and looking at the two young men in front of me, what they had achieved and how they lived their lives, made me a very proud father.

I spent the majority of the next day in bed. My back pain had returned with a vengeance. Rory spent the day with me, making sure I was comfortable and bringing me my medication. He then did something I never dreamt I would ever do, he introduced me to box set television shows. The only things that interested me on TV were the news and sports channels. Now and again, I was under Kim's order to watch series like 'Downton Abbey' and a few others I really cannot recall. I must confess, I did enjoy most of them.

This was different. I was about to get hooked onto series which had been running for many seasons and I could binge on them. He started me off with 'Making a Murderer' and that was it. I watched series after series over the months that followed, my favourite being 'Breaking Bad'. I even have the mug and t-shirt to prove it.

Getting back to the present, Ryan had made an appointment for me to visit the GP the following day. It was his turn to stay with me and we made our way to the surgery on foot. It was located less than a kilometer from his flat. Being on a slight incline, I shuffled my way there, armed with my blood tests results and medical report from South Africa, as well as a list of all of the medication I was on.

After filling in a couple of forms, I went through to the doctor. I was greeted by Dr Powell, another young doctor with a kind and likeable face. I explained my situation and she went through my records.

"Your PSA numbers are extremely high," she says, looking directly at me. "This indicates cancer of the prostate. Your back pain is also a serious concern."

She explained that they could not rely on the South African tests and would need to do their own. In the meantime she would 'fast track' me to see a Urologist. This would take two weeks and I would be contacted directly from the Urology department at Southmead Hospital.

She went through my list of medicines and felt that they were not strong enough for the pain I was experiencing, so I was prescribed stronger ones. I was introduced to Tramadol, a strong painkiller which I had to take four times per day, along with paracetamols and a pill for nausea. Along with these, I had to wear a morphine patch on my upper arm. After having my blood taken, Ryan and I cautiously made our way back to his flat, stopping halfway downhill at the chemist, to pick up the prescriptions. Would this, at long last, be the end of my suffering?

Wishful thinking.

The weekend came and went and the back pain persisted, worsened even, with the new medication. It was becoming more and more difficult to be mobile and I was fortunate to have the boys to assist me with simple chores like getting in and out of bed. With the new drugs, also came the side effects. I began bringing up and lost my appetite completely. I also started to have vertigo and was now very unstable on my feet. My weight loss was becoming noticeable.

The following Sunday, after having spent an awful week, the pain became intolerable. The boys called the medical emergency number and explained my situation. On checking my medical record, they recommended that I should take morphine orally. They sent the prescription directly to a pharmacy in the city centre. Ryan rushed there and was back with the morphine within minutes, but it seemed like hours to me. I took an initial dosage of 10ml, followed by additional doses of 2.5ml every four hours. It tasted vile, but it worked. At long last some relief.

The worst, however, was was still to come. The following Tuesday morning, I was woken from my normal disturbed sleep at about 4.30am. Lying on my back, it felt like my spinal column was about to explode. I was in a cold sweat in a drenched t-shirt. I could not move my arms or legs. I called out to Ryan, but could only make a whimpering sound, too feeble for him to hear. I just laid quietly in the dark, tolerating a type of pain I had never felt before. I heard Ryan coughing lightly in his sleep. I took a deep breath and called out to him as loudly as I could. Within seconds, he was by my side.

"What's the matter Dad?" He asks anxiously, holding my hand. "Gosh, your hands are ice cold. have you taken your medication?"

"I can't move." I whisper back to him. "This pain is killing me and I can hardly breathe."

He propped me up on a pile of pillows and helped me to swallow a couple of Tramadols.

"Let's give this a little while," he said, "then you will need to take some morphine."

"I will call the doctor's room the moment it opens," he assured me.

A few minutes later, he helped me take the morphine, but the pain persisted and my chest felt tight.

It was now nearly six in the morning and concerned, he called Rory. Within fifteen minutes, Rory arrived, after running all the way from his flat. My condition did not improve and they decided to call the emergency services. On describing my condition, they were told that the Paramedics were on their way. The response was swift. Within ten minutes of the call, an ambulance pulled up outside of the flat. Two paramedics enter the bedroom and after a quick check, told me that I was completely dehydrated and that my heart rate and shortness of breath were a major concern.

Within minutes, I was hooked up to an electrocardiogram machine and an intravenous line was inserted into my upper arm. They proceeded by forcing fluids into my vein, at least three types, the last one being 20ml of morphine. They then connected the line to a very large IV fluid bag for rehydration. They sat on each side of me, one constantly checking my blood pressure, while the other held onto my wrists for pulse rates.

It was then that I looked up and saw both boys, at the bedroom door, watching anxiously as the Paramedics worked on me. I felt sad and annoyed that they had to witness me going through so much trauma. The Paramedics assured me that the pain would soon recede. They were correct and within a couple of minutes, the pain slowly but surely eases. I give the boys a thumbs up and a smile. The crisis was over.

Because of the condition they had found me in, they insisted on taking me to the hospital for a full check-up. We waited another fifteen minutes for me to get some strength back. Ryan and Rory dressed me and with me holding on to both of them, we gingerly make our way to the ambulance. The Paramedics enquired which one of my sons would accompany me and they reply that they both would. With that, the ambulance, loaded with the three of us, speeds to the city centre, sirens blazing.

Within minutes, we had reached the Bristol Infirmary and I was speedily admitted through to the emergency department. The day unfolded with me being fed more morphine and IV drips and being taken for x-rays. I was visited by a specialist nurse from the Oncology department and I informed her that I had an appointment with a Urologist at Southmead Hospital in a week's time.

After consultation between her and the doctor who took care of me, it was agreed that all that they could do was help me as best they could in managing the pain until my visit with the Urologist. Ryan and Rory stayed by my side the whole time. We decided not to tell their Mother, who messaged them regularly, about what had happened. She had enough on her plate and would be with us soon enough anyway.

Ryan had brought along with him a list which he had made of all of the medications that I was on, as well as a log that they had kept of the times and at what intervals I took the medicines. The doctor was suitably impressed at how well organised they were. Due to the crippling pain I was now experiencing, coupled with breakthrough pain, he re-arranged the schedule and dosage, which had to be strictly adhered to, until my Urology appointment. I was now on 27 tablets per day, as well as increased strength morphine patches and liquid morphine to be taken orally. Later that evening, I was discharged from hospital and walked out with the boys by my side.

***

I had a mid-week appointment with the GP and she was concerned with my weight loss of over 10kgs over the past four months. I felt weak, had no appetite and despite the nausea tablets, I was now bringing up regularly. She prescribed a vitamin enriched nutritional supplement that had to be mixed with full cream milk and drunk as a shake, twice daily. I did my best, but it was near impossible to keep it down. The pain persisted and my only solution was to become pain defiant until I met up with the Urologist.

The day of my appointment had arrived. It was on a bank holiday Monday. The Urology clinic was situated at Southmead Hospital. A large and modern hospital, newly built in the northern suburb of Bristol. Walking into any hospital has always been an unpleasant experience for me, but the entrance and appearance of this building completely demystified this feeling and I felt relaxed. It had a huge atrium that ran the whole length of the building and made you feel you were in a holiday resort. It would take me at least twenty minutes to walk the length of this building and as the Urology clinic was at the end of it, a motorised buggy was thankfully made available to take us to our destination.

Everything was computerised. You recorded your arrival at a 'self check-in kiosk at the main entrance and it directed you to your waiting area, which was furnished with comfortable chairs for you to wait in until your name appeared on a large screen, telling you which room to go to. This was a well organised and highly professional establishment.

Once in the clinic, we were met by a nurse who accompanied us to a large consulting room, informing us that the Urologist would be with us shortly. True to her word, the doctor soon walks in, clutching a medical file. He is a well built man, sporting a neatly trimmed beard and moustache.

After the customary greetings, he sits at the desk opposite me. From his accent, I assume that he is Canadian.

"What are you here for?" He asks, staring at me. "What can we do for you?"

Here we go again, I think to myself. He has my file in front of him, and I need to go through this whole painful process again.

"Is it not all explained in my records?" I reply, pointing to the file laying on the desk.

"I have not looked at your file." He says sternly, holding my gaze. "I need you to tell me in detail, why you are here and what is wrong with you."

I knew then that I was not going to win this little battle, even though I felt that he had gone through my medical records and was well aware of my condition. Feeling a little irritated, I proceed to tell him in as much detail as possible of my condition, going back to January when my back pains began. I made sure not to miss out on the important points.

He stares at me the whole time, not once interrupting. Ryan was sitting next to me and Rory remained standing behind the two of us. When I had finished, he began speaking in softer tones and I immediately sensed that this was an expert, with many, many years of experience.

"The PSA reading we took recently shows that it has gone up by twenty points, compared to the one taken in South Africa."

So he has seen my records, I was right all along.

"There is no no doubt in my mind. There is a high probability that you have metastatic prostate cancer."

"I am also aware that you were recently admitted at the Bristol Royal Infirmary and that your back pain still persists, despite the amount of medication you've been given. I will now arrange for you to have urgent bone scans, but as from today, you will begin hormonal therapy."

He goes on to explain, at length, the mechanism of action of hormone therapy and all of it's side effects. He would also request my GP to take additional blood tests and promised that he would introduce me to a specialist nurse, who would from then on be my point of contact.

"Now for your prognosis," he goes on. "From what you've told me and the pain you've described, I believe the cancer has spread to your bones. Without the scans, I am not aware to what extent. With us starting the hormonal therapy immediately, which will be a life long treatment, I would say that your life expectancy could be between five to eight years."

He had hardly finished the sentence and his words were only beginning to sink in, when I see Ryan jump from his seat. Rory had turned snow white. After sitting down for a few minutes with his face in the palm of his hands, close to his knees, he recovers.

Once fully recovered, the Urologist speaks to both the boys, stressing to them the importance of them having a PSA test done, on a yearly basis, once they reach forty years of age.
"If detected at an early stage, prostate cancer can now be easily treated, with an excellent success rate," he tells them.

With that, we shake hands warmly and leave the consulting room, armed with the prescription for my hormone therapy and various booklets to read on the matter.
Holding on to the arms of my boys, walking alongside me, we slowly make our way back to the buggy waiting patiently to take us back to the entrance of the hospital.

"With the pain I was experiencing," I tell the boys, "I was expecting this diagnosis. As for the prognosis, that's another matter."

"Don't worry Dad," they reply. "You will beat this. We are in this fight together."

CHAPTER NINE
BAD NEWS IS BAD NEWS

Kim would be arriving in a couple of days.

I had gone through the various booklets and brochures which the Urologist had given to me in fine detail. As he had explained, hormone therapy on it's own was not a cure for prostate cancer. It keeps it under control, sometimes for several years, before further treatments such as chemotherapy or radiotherapy become necessary.

Hormone therapy shrinks the cancer and slows its growth, even if it has spread. How long it will control the cancer varies from man to man, depending on various factors such as the aggressiveness of the cancer, as well as the physical condition and overall health of the patient. This makes it difficult for doctors to give an accurate prognosis. This therapy also comes with side effects that will affect you for as long as you're on it. In my case, the remainder of my life. The common side effects being hot flushes, fatigue, strength and muscle loss, bone thinning and loss of body hair. Less common effects will be memory loss, mood changes and the inability to concentrate. The latter certainly not applying to me, being more than halfway writing this book.

It was a lot to take in. The pros and cons of such a therapy began playing on my mind. I had done a fair amount of research and read numerous articles on alternative cancer treatments. Where do I place my faith? It was either the scientific way, or the holistic way. I had followed, with intense interest, the arguments both for and against natural cures for cancer. I was amazed by the amount of sufferers that felt holistic cancer therapy was the right approach. What surprised me the most, was the amount of natural cures offered. These cures ranged from various types of vitamins to the consumption of medicinal mushrooms, ginger, marijuana and many more. You could even get admitted into a holistic cancer treatment centre for a course of treatment. What also astonished me, were the amount of products for sale on the internet which claimed that they could cure your cancer. In my personal opinion, these were all dubious, untested products offered with the sole intention of getting desperate sufferers to part with their cash.

At that stage, I also had long discussions with my brother, Christian, a huge advocate and believer in the benefits of vitamins supplement. His champion was the renowned American professor Linus Pauling, a double Nobel prize winner, who claimed that mega doses of vitamin C had preventative and curative effects on diseases such as cancer and aids. Both Christian and his lovely wife, Danielle, are walking examples of good health and they simply put it down to the copious amount of vitamins which they consume daily. I must stress that at no stage did Christian suggest that vitamins alone could cure me. However, he was adamant that I could use vitamins as part of my fighting arsenal, along with whatever therapies the Oncologists recommended. In other words, combat this vile disease with both science and nature.

My mind was made up. I would go the scientific way and put all of my energy and trust in the expertise and knowledge of the Specialists. I would go along with whatever treatment and therapies these highly educated Professionals recommended. But permanently by my side, will be a large tube of 1000mg vitamin C and I will be popping them down my throat at regular intervals.

The following day, I began therapy. I commenced initially with Bicalutamide tablets for a period of seven days, before my first injection of LHRH, short for Luteinizing hormone releasing hormone agonists, whatever that meant. It's job was to stop the manufacture of testosterone and as prostate cancer cells need testosterone to grow, it would starve it and keep it under control.

At about the same time, I received notification from the Oncology centre at Bristol Royal Infirmary, stating that I also needed to have a full MRI scan. I remember that experience only too well. It was the first time I had a scan and I found the whole procedure of being in such a tight and confined space extremely claustrophobic and unpleasant. As usual, both Ryan and Rory accompanied me to the hospital and on the way back, I began to feel nauseous. We reached our destination just in time. I stumbled out of the car and was violently sick on the pavement, under the shocked and relieved gaze of the Uber driver. Feeling weak and exhausted, Ryan carries me to the apartment, where he feeds me my meds with an extra nausea tablet for good measure.

***

Kim lands in Bristol a day later. I could tell by the expression on her face that she was shocked and taken aback at my physical appearance. During the past two weeks, I had lost more weight due to no interest in food intake and my skin had turned a yellowish tone. I shuffled about like an old person and had permanent dark circles under my eyes. I remember her telling me that it did not matter what I looked like on the outside, I will always be the same person on the inside. She always said the right things in the calmness way. It was exactly what I needed to hear that day.

It was great to have her by my side again. I was also pleased that the boys could resume their normal lives. The care, love and support which they had given me this past, long fortnight is something which will stay with me forever. They were my champions.

As I had left South Africa in such a hurry, Kim filled me in on the events of the past weeks, which had been emotionally draining for her as well. In that space of time, she had sold the furniture and whatever was not sold was sent to an auction house. We had to let go of many pieces of furniture, objects and artwork that were precious and of great sentimental value to us. Most of it purchased on our travels. She packed all of the items which she felt we could not part with in boxes, to be shipped at a later stage. A suitable tenant was found to take over our lease and at the end of August, she vacated the little simplex where we had spent a tremendously happy couple of years.

So much change had been forced on her because of my illness, but as per her usual self, she handled it all in her inimitable calm way. Since getting back to Durban, she had re-ignited old friendships and spent valuable time with her girlfriends, walking along the esplanades and sharing many coffee mornings. She knew also, whether forced on us or not, that we were all about to be united again as a family, and that was a great blessing to her.

Thankfully, Kim now took full control of my care. I had reached the stage where I could no longer do simple everyday activities such as getting in and out of the shower, washing my hair or get dressed.

Within a week of starting the hormone pills, I felt a marked improvement in my mobility. The pain began subsiding and I also slept better. I was able to walk unaided to the local surgery for my first LHRH injection.

***

A few days later, I was to attend the Imaging section at Southmead Hospital for a nuclear medicine scan. This was a lengthy procedure. On arrival, I was given an NM injection, a radioactive tracer injected in my vein by a radiographer. I would then need to wait three hours between the injection and the scan. The size of the syringe and needle of this 'nuclear' injection was not for the faint hearted. With it also comes a caution that once administered, I should not have contact with young children and pregnant women for a period of twenty-four hours, as I could expose them to radiation.

After spending three hours in the coffee shop situated in the lobby, indulging in overpriced cups of coffee and hot chocolate, it was time for the scan. I was anxious, thinking of my previous experience in a scanner. I need not have worried. In this instance, you lie flat on a bed and the images are taken by a machine called a gamma camera. As you are scanned, the images appear on a widescreen monitor which, for whatever reason, was turned towards me. I saw my skeletal form and it looked as though it was decorated with very bright Christmas lights. The Radiographer, noticing that I was staring at the screen, very diplomatically turned it away from my gaze. I remember talking to Don about it a few days after the scan. He dismissed it as being insignificant and very quickly changed the subject to the rampart form of the mighty Chelsea Football team. Even so, the image of this illumination stayed with me. surely it meant something.

Thankfully, with the hormone injection, my back pain had become a mere ache. Around this time, the side effects started kicking in, especially hot flushes and fatigue. I felt weak and lacked energy. Appointments with Urologists and Oncologists began streaming in. My next one being with an oncology specialist nurse at Southmead Hospital. After discussing in great detail how I was responding to the hormone treatment, she suggested that I should undergo a prostate biopsy. As it was obvious that the cancer had spread, it could be to my advantage if I was invited to take part in some form of clinical trial. Being on such a trial had huge advantages, she explained, the obvious one being that I would be monitored very closely and offered new treatments, as and when they became available. Without a biopsy, I would not qualify and would never be offered this opportunity. After having been explained the procedure of a prostate biopsy, I agreed to it immediately. She left the consulting room and five minutes later returned, saying that I could have the biopsy done the very next day and that they would call me with a time. They were now pushing things along at a furious pace.

The next day we made our way back to Southmead for the procedure. It was scheduled for two in the afternoon and Rory came along with us. We made our way to the 'Urology day case' department and after the usual registration routine, we were shown to the treatment room. The consultant and a nurse soon joined us. He introduced himself and went into detail about the procedure. He also took time to talk about my condition. He had come across many cases very similar to mine. I pushed him for a prognosis and he replied that it all depended on the spread and aggressiveness of the cancer, but from experience, I had a maximum of five years to live. I should have kept my trap shut. Serves me right. I glance across at Rory, expecting him to fall off of his chair, but this time he does not flinch. On leaving the treatment room, he gives Kim and Rory a long handshake, telling them that although this was a difficult period for them, they could rest assured that we were now part of their family and that I would get the best care possible.

The biopsy itself was a lot more uncomfortable than I had imagined. A fairly large object is pushed up your back passage and at the end of it, some sort of stapler removes six samples of tissue from your prostate gland. Even with the surrounding area having been injected with an anaesthetic to minimise the discomfort, I felt an electric shock run through my body every time a piece of tissue was collected. Once done, and due to the bleeding, you are handed sets of pads that you change into at regular intervals, until the bleeding stops. Only then are you discharged and free to go home. Not a pleasant day out.

The tissue samples would now be sent to a laboratory to be examined by a Pathologist. He will determine the Gleason score, a method developed in the sixties which helps to predict the aggressiveness of the cancer, by means of cancer cell patterns in your tissue samples. The result of the test would then be sent directly to my Oncologist within a week.

＊

It was nearing the end of September and we were due a visit from my niece Mylene. She had flown to London on business and found the time to spend a couple of days with us in Bristol. She brought with her lots of heart warming and positive messages from Durban. Amongst it all, she also brought me a Scapular, sent to me by my good friend Michel. The Scapula is a Christian garment, worn over the shoulders, which reminds the person wearing it of his commitment to Christian life. It also helps to remove the burden which you carry on your shoulders. I was very happy to wear it, a privilege in fact. The Catholic Church, however, sees the reason behind wearing a Scapular a little differently. I will discuss that along with another utterly interesting story at a latter stage. Anyway, it was a wonderful feeling to know that so many people back home were rooting for me and praying for my recovery. We spent a great couple of days with Mylene. I felt strong enough to go out to a restaurant for lunch, where we were joined by the boys and their girlfriends. We spent the evening playing games and watching football. No game boards or tables got flipped over. The next day, I had a long rest, as I had an early appointment with my GP the following day.

As per usual, Kim and I made our way on foot to the surgery, with me stopping every fifty meters or so for a breather. Once there, I made my way to the consulting room, where the GP performs her routine check ups. After taking my blood pressure and assessing my weight, we discuss the side effects which I was beginning to experience from the hormone therapy and how best to manage them. Then, glancing at her computer screen, she tells me that all of my results were in and that I had been diagnosed. She goes on saying that she could discuss it with me, or I could wait until the end of the week and discuss it with the Oncologist.

"I will be happy to hear it from you." I tell her. "The sooner I know, the better."

"Unfortunately, it's not very good news." She says, her eyes glued to the screen.

"You have been diagnosed with stage 4 cancer," she goes on. "The cancer has spread to the bones and you have multiple skeletal metastases in your ribs, thorax, lumbar spine, sacrum and left proximal femur."

I just sit there, dazed and deep in thought. After a lifetime of good health, never having to spend a single day in a hospital, this body of mine has now really betrayed me. That haunting image of my skeleton all lit up races through my mind.

This is it. I am riddled with the stuff and this is the reason for the unbearable amount of pain I've been enduring for months.

"What does stage 4 mean?" I ask, hoping desperately for an answer which would soften the blow. Not to be.

"Stage 4 cancer is the highest stage you can reach." she goes on. "It just means that it has spread from where it originated, to other parts of your body. It's also referred to as secondary or metastatic cancer."

"What are the chances of survival?" I ask, thinking of Kim, sitting in the waiting room, unaware of the trauma I was going through.

"Once you reach stage 4, there is sadly no cure." she says honestly. "However, there are excellent treatments out there to prolong your life. Your Oncologist will discuss all of that with you. There are many factors at play here." She says, "and to give an accurate prognosis will prove difficult. I will leave that to them."

That was that. We discuss a few other issues, mainly my diet, as my weight loss had concerned her. Before leaving, she kindly tells me that although she had only met with me on a couple of occasions, she was impressed with my state of mind and positivity and felt I had all the attributes to fight this disease head on. I thanked her and make my way back to the waiting room to break the news to my wife.

***

Kim and I walked slowly downhill, back to the apartment. We stop halfway for her to run into a small metro supermarket and grab a couple of items. I sit on the bench outside. It's freezing but I was well covered and enjoyed breathing in the cold air, watching the sun desperately trying to break through the grey autumn clouds. I decided to tell her about the diagnosis on the remainder of our journey to the flat. As we resume our walk, I told her what the doctor had said in as much detail as I can. Glancing over at her, I noticed that there was no change in her facial expression except for a couple of small teardrops gently creeping down the side of her cheek. I gave her hand a gentle squeeze and we carried on walking quietly to the front door.

The first thing we do back home is make a cup of tea. It always amazes me how much better and clearer everything becomes when discussed over a brew. Like me, the news had knocked her back, but only temporarily. Having witnessed first hand the suffering I had experienced these past months, she was prepared for the worse. We now knew what laid ahead of us and it was imperative to stay focussed and positive. I was very fortunate that I was going to get the best care possible. That evening, we discuss the diagnosis with the boys and they also react maturely and positively to it. As a family, we had a tough challenge ahead of us, but we were ready to meet it head on. Strangely enough, I slept well that night and woke up the next morning without a single trace of anxiety.

As the family back in Durban were anxiously waiting for the results of my tests, I sent an e-mail to my sister, Marielle, breaking the news to her with as much positivity I could muster. To alleviate any confusion, we've always called ourselves by our nicknames. She is Yel and I am Dioul.

On the same day I receive her heartbreaking but positive response.

It reads as follows:

Hello from a very sad Durban.

Hi Dioul,

This is very sad news. Deep inside I knew that this was what I was going to hear. You've suffered too much, and for too long Dioul. How I wish I was near you right now.

I can't believe how positive you remain. You were right when you told me that you thought the cancer had spread to your bones and legs. I've prayed so hard and will carry on praying. You will do well with the hormone injections.

All I can tell you Dioul, is that I cannot imagine a world without you in it, so you better stay positive and carry on fighting.

I am devastated but will carry on praying and sending positive thoughts your way.

Big hugs to Kim, Ryan and Rory,

I love you lots,
Yel

To which I reply:

Thanks so much for your kindness and love Yel.

I was expecting the worst, so it did not come as a shock.
My body has been telling me for a long time now that I had something serious. We will need to see what sort of treatment I will be offered and take it from there.

There is now no possibility of a cure, but there is absolutely no way that I'll ever give up. I will fight this with all of my might and prolong my life for as long as possible.

Don't be sad, just keep sending positive thoughts my way.

Love you tons,
Dioul.

CHAPTER TEN
NOT GOING ANYWHERE

The hormone therapy was working well, reducing these horrendous back pains to just unpleasant aches. However, along with this came the usual side effects. I also became tired far too easily. For instance, it became increasingly more difficult to walk up a small incline to the grocery store. I often felt light headed and unbalanced. I would now not dare to venture out on my own. I needed Kim constantly by my side.

At the end of September, I received word from the Oncology unit at Bristol Royal Infirmary. Before meeting with me, they wanted me to undergo an additional series of CT scans, concentrating on my chest, abdomen, and pelvis with contrast. All of these tests were scheduled for the following Saturday morning at 8.00am. As per usual, Kim and I made our way there with the ever reliable service of Uber. The thoughts running through my mind on the way there were of the unpleasant feeling of being trapped in this long dark tunnel, accompanied by very loud noises.

I need not have worried. A CT scanner is a ring like structure and you pass through it while laying down. The Radiographer who carried out the scan went to great length explaining to me that the CT scan, a very complex and special type of x-ray machine, is connected to a computer that produces cross-sectional images of your body. I also learnt that day that the letters CT stood for computerised tomography.

The results of these fresh tests would take a couple of days. A few days later both, Kim and I made our way back to the hospital and, for the first time, to the Bristol Haematology and Oncology Centre, located on the fifth floor of a tall building behind the Bristol Infirmary. We did not have to wait long before being shown to a consulting room.

A bespectacled Consultant greeted us. Soft spoken and with the kindest of faces, he slowly and purposefully went through all of the test results with me. Also in the room with us was an uro-oncology nurse, who simply introduced herself as Lucy. He told me that as well as my scans, they had also received the results of my biopsy. My Gleason score was a 3:4, which meant that the cancer had not reached its most aggressive state. The CT scans showed that it had not spread to any of my vital organs.

This is going well, I thought to myself. Looking across at Kim, I give her a wink and a large grin. Both were soon to be wiped from my face. With that speck of good news also comes the bad news. The dreaded prognosis. He felt that I had one to three years to live. I was speechless. Again, I glanced over at Kim, this time she had her head down staring at her hands, neatly folded in her lap. We both tried to come to terms with what we'd just been told. I was now becoming a little agitated and tired of these forever changing prognosis.

"Really? That is really incredible." I say, almost sarcastically. "Every time I am given a prognosis, it gets worse and worse. This is now my third prognosis. I suppose the next one will give me six months to live? I am sorry Doctor, but I am not going anywhere."

There you are, I thought to myself, I've said what had to be said.

I sat there, defiantly staring at this highly educated and professional man, waiting and hoping for a retraction to what he had just told me. Not a chance. Instead, he went on calmly to inform me that huge strides were being made in this field at the moment. He told me that once he had completed a few checks, he wanted me to meet another person. After performing a series of arms and legs tests to determine what strength I still possessed, he left the consulting room and returned a couple of minutes later with another bespectacled gentleman. He introduced himself as Nick Robbins, a clinical trials unit research nurse. He informed me that they had reviewed my case and that they would like to invite me to participate in a clinical trial called 'STAMPEDE', which stood for 'Systemic Therapy in Advancing or Metastatic Prostate Cancer Evaluation of Drug Efficacy'.

He explained that the study looked at adding new and different treatments to the standard way in which my cancer was currently being managed. This could enable me to live longer and have a better quality of life. I would need to undergo additional tests and a blood test to make sure that I did not have diabetes. He informed me that these trials were under the control of the Medical Research Council, and funded by Cancer Research UK. Glancing at Kim, the expression on her face reflected how I felt. In our darkest hour, I was hopefully being thrown some sort of a lifeline. Not a cure, but at least more ammunition with which to fight this dreadful enemy. It was a no brainer and I immediately told him that I would be more than happy to participate.

Nick and the Oncologist went on to explain that if my screening tests returned positive, the first step of the trial would be for me to undergo a series of chemotherapy cycles at the same time as hormone therapy. This had to start as soon as possible. With that, Nick took me to an adjoining room and took some additional blood samples. He handed me a wad of literature to read about the trial, as well as a consent form to go through carefully before signing. He assured me that he would call me as soon as he had the results and if all was okay, I needed to get the signed forms to him as soon as possible. This would make me a participant in all aspects of this clinical trial. After saying warm goodbyes to the Oncologist, Lucy, and Nick, Kim and I left the building feeling positive that I was in very good hands and in the best of care. I felt blessed.

As promised, a day or so later I received a phone call from Nick Robbins, giving me the good news that all of the tests were positive. He asked me to call in as soon as possible to undergo an ECG and sign all of the consent forms. This was done and I was soon sent the scheduled dates for my chemotherapy. It would begin on the 1st November 2016 and would be repeated six times, every three weeks, ending on 14th February 2017. It also indicated that each session would last at least four hours. Prior to the first session, I was to attend a chemotherapy informative session. This was booked for the end of October.

***

Having a couple of weeks to spare before the commencement of my first chemo session, Kim and I began our search for a place to live. We had more than overstayed our welcome at Ryan's. We needed to let the poor fellow have his life and bedroom back. Having done a little research, we felt that the Clifton, Redlands area would be a great location to live in. Everything we looked at in that area sadly proved far too pricey. Ideally, we were looking for a one bedroom ground floor flat, as anything with stairs would be too demanding on my back. A bonus would be a wet room and some sort of medical emergency system. Kim searched the internet and e-mailed dozens of establishments, explaining my situation and what we were looking for.

Out of the blue, we receive a response from a lady named Diane, the resident manager of an apartment unit situated in the heart of Clifton. With it being walking distances to a medical surgery, shops, a chemist, bus stops and a beautiful park, it met all of our criterias, even including the wet room and medical help system. Kim and Rory gave the property a viewing and both felt that I would find the living space much too small. A day or so later, on one of my 'good' days, I went back with Kim and immediately liked the feel of the place. We signed a lease agreement and after purchasing a few pieces of furniture and a comfortable bed, we were set to move in at the beginning of the following month.

***

At the end of October, Kim and I attended the chemography informative session at the Oncology centre. Walking into a large room full of people, you could immediately spot the sufferers. Like me, their appearance had visibly been affected, mainly by weight loss but more so by the discoloration of their skin. The brochure handed to us prior to arriving explained the aim of this session to us. Over and above providing us with essential information about chemotherapy and its side effects, we would also be told about the specific drug which would be given to us. I counted eight patients and like me they were accompanied by a family member. The majority of them were much younger than I was and all had that anxious and sad look engraved on their faces.

What a nasty, ruthless and unforgiving disease cancer is.

The talk was expertly delivered by a specialist nurse and the information she shared was very thorough. She spoke at length about how chemotherapy works and how it is administered. A full blood count test needed to be carried out before each session and if the Oncologist was not satisfied with the result, the session would be cancelled. She then went into details about the side effects and the risk of infection.

Suddenly, the nurse stopped speaking and stared directly at me. Only then did I notice that Kim had turned as white as a sheet, with her head drooped over her chest. Oh no, here we go again, I think to myself. Another fainter. So that's where Rory gets it from.

"Is she alright?" enquired the nurse, knowing that I was the patient and it was my wife who was about to pass out.

The nurse brought her some water and after a few sips and resting her head between her knees, under the glare of everyone around us, she recovered. The nurse resumed her talk, but kept a beady eye on Kim for the remainder of the session. This little episode, as well as previous ones, made me realise how this whole cancer business has affected my family.

It really saddens me, but also makes me angry and more determined than ever to beat this beast.

At the end of the nurse's session, we were given talks by amiable volunteers from various organisations, such as Cancer research UK, MacMillan Cancer Support and Cancer advice UK. I was amazed at the amount of support which these organisations provided, in terms of both practical and emotional needs. They left us with their contact numbers, as well as informative literature and insisted that we called them if we needed any advice, as well as financial help or guidance. They would also help with items like wigs, special protein food, body massages and makeup sessions for the ladies.

I then had a one on one consultation with the specialist nurse. This was when I was told that the drug I would be given was Docetaxel. I was given a leaflet outlining it's common side effects. At a quick glance, I counted nineteen. The ones that caught my immediate attention were hair loss, vomiting, bleeding nose and gums, fatigue and irregular bladder and bowel movements - charming. Not much to be too concerned about then. We left the hospital armed with a bunch of drugs to be taken before my first cycle, the main ones being steroids and anti-sickness tablets.

***

The day of my first session had arrived. I was warned that I would feel anxious and on edge and it would be normal to feel stressed. I strangely felt completely the opposite to that. To me, chemotherapy was simply an important task which had to be accomplished. From this moment onwards, I had to show grit, resilience and determination. Watch and admire, I will blow this disease away with my mental toughness. With these positive thoughts in mind, Kim and I walked confidently into the chemotherapy unit.

We were welcomed by a charming senior nurse and made to feel very relaxed and comfortable. The room itself was L shaped, with a capacity of treating twenty-five patients at a time. Rows of comfortable recliners were placed alongside each other on either side of a large aisle. Each station had it's own monitors, and I noticed that all were armed with a panic button. Once made comfortable in my recliner, with Kim sitting opposite me, the nurse and her assistant go to work.

I had been awake pretty much the whole night on a steroid induced high. I had taken my usual set of painkillers that morning, enough to make my stomach rattle. I now had to swallow more pills. A wristband was attached to my right wrist, written on it was my personal information and in large letters: DOCETAXEL - CYCLE ONE. Here we go.

The kind nurse took my blood pressure and once satisfied, inserted a nasty needle into one of my accomodating veins, in my left hand. This was connected to an IV line. First a saline solution was pumped into me, followed by my first dose of toxic drug, hooked above me and connected to a pump that regulated its flow into my body. Whilst all of this took place, the assistant nurse ran through a whole set of medication with Kim for us to take home, one of these being an injection called Zarzio. It's objective is to stimulate the production of white blood cells. I needed to self-inject myself in the stomach for the next seven days. It comes with an information booklet that would hopefully teach one how to inject oneself. The instructions are fairly simple: remove the syringe from the refrigerator; don't shake it; choose an injection site on your abdomen except for the two inch area around your belly button; check syringe for air bubbles; clean the selected skin area with an alcohol pad; insert the needle in one quick motion at a 90 degree angle; once in slowly push the plunger all the way down; once empty, pull the syringe out of your stomach. Presto, mission accomplished, just like that. Easy.

The morning was progressing well. Kim had gone to get herself a cup of coffee and I sat quietly, watching the poison enter my body, drip by drip. Then suddenly, it started happening. A patient a couple of seats away from me hit her panic button. Within seconds she had a bunch of nurses rushing to her station, drawing the curtains around her. A couple of minutes later another panic button was activated and more nurses rush to the patient's aid. More panic buttons are activated and the ward was now abuzz with doctors and nurses. Kim had returned with her beverage and we both sat there, amazed at the immense commotion around us. We heard a nurse at the other end shouting 'cardiac arrest' and the station number.

I held onto my panic button, assuming it would be my turn soon. Nothing happened. I felt no different to how I had felt walking in there. A couple of hours later my fluid bag was empty. At that stage, calm had been restored in the unit. Many patients had their session stopped and were either sent home or to another unit to be cared for. The nurse removed the needle from my hand, checked my blood pressure one more time and declared that all was well and I could go home. She gave Kim an emergency number, in case I felt unwell and developed a high temperature in the days ahead. I thanked the nurses for their care and we walked out of the unit. 'This is a breeze,' I think to myself.

It was now a couple of days after the chemo and all was well. Food, as expected, began tasting like cardboard. Even water had a particularly horrible taste. I was beginning to get used to the hot flushes and the sleeplessness caused by the steroids. And then it hit me. It was a Friday evening, three days after the treatment. Every bone and joint in my body began aching. I had a headache that did not let up and began having nosebleeds. I sweated heavily and the perspiration pouring out of me had a strong chemical smell. I was nauseous and began vomiting as well as dragging myself to the bathroom at regular intervals with diarrhoea. I prayed for a few hours of sleep and some relief from this dreadful feeling, but the steroids denied me that. There was no escape route and it gradually got worse over the weekend. I lay in a dark room, hoping that my condition would soon improve, but it did not. I could not look at food, nevermind consume anything. I felt permanently nauseous and clearly had absolutely nothing left to bring up.

By the Monday morning, I could hardly move or speak. My voice had been reduced to a murmur. Kim called the emergency number she was given and on describing my condition, they said I had to come in immediately. To this day, I still cannot recall how I made it to the Oncology Emergency Unit. The nurses took one look at me and within minutes I was on a bed, attached to a drip and made to swallow a large dose of steroids tablets as well as oral morphine. The Oncologist who I had my first appointment with came up to see me and after a few checks, told me that I had to have an MRI the following day. He felt that the dosage which they had given me on the first cycle was too strong and it would have to be adjusted for future chemo sessions. I was kept on a drip for the rest of the afternoon as I was completely dehydrated and I was fed even more steroids. Early that evening, I began feeling a lot better. A couple of hours later, I was discharged from hospital and was able to walk, pain free, for the first time in three days.

The very next morning, I had my MRI at the Bristol Infirmary and waited until the afternoon for the results and a further consultation with the Oncologist. He declared that all was stable and that the therapies were doing their jobs. A week later, I was advised by the Oncologist that the strength of the dosage would be reduced by twenty percent. This would make no difference to the treatment. I was also advised that my PSA levels had dropped considerably to 2.7. My previous reading was 260.0 plus. I was very pleased with myself and after the consultation, as I normally did, I dropped Don an e-mail, giving him the news.

This is what he emailed me back:

Hi Gil,

Wozza.
How is the warrior today?
These prostate cancer cells are getting a beating and starved of their androgen/ testosterone food, by the hormones blocking off their supply at the cellular level. The chemo also doing it's work. Beautiful science in action. That is why research is so important.

Thanks be to the Lord. Never discount Him.

Love,
Don

This email, alongside the dozens of goodwill messages and calls that I was receiving from my family back home, were constant reminders that I was not alone in this fight. It was now time to dominate this disease.

My second chemo cycle went as well as the first one. The unit was very quiet on this occasion, with nobody pushing their panic buttons. The only difference this time was that I feel a slight tightening in my chest, and had to advise the nurse. She slowed down the flow of the chemo and after a short while, all was well.

After the session, Kim and I took our leisurely ten minute walk down to the town centre. The Christmas decorations were up and the market stalls, resembling Swiss chalets, had been set up along the High Street. They offer a variety of products, including Mulled wine, served warm and combined with spices, as well as roasted chestnuts and caramelised nuts. The sound of carols filled the cold air and thousands of lights twinkled from giant Christmas trees. We found a bench and basked in this wonderful atmosphere of good cheer, joy and hope. I felt good.

***

It was 1st December 2016 and with the help of our sons and their girlfriends, we moved into our small flat in Clifton. We were made to feel very welcomed by Diane, the complex manager, as well as the neighbour living above us, a jovial retired Welsh dental Professor by the name of John. He welcomed and spoiled us with a beautiful, freshly assembled Christmas wreath as well as a bunch of flowers. He was delighted to hear that I had lived in South Africa and Wales and like him, have a great love for sports, especially rugby.

Dianne on the other hand, is a diehard Bristol Rovers fan and loves talking football. I now had two delightful individuals in the building to have a good natter with. Kim, as per her usual self, made our little flat 'bijou like' and very comfortable. Over the next couple of weeks, we got to meet the other residents and they are all lovely. Living in the desirable suburb of Clifton was great. With its wealth of Victorian and Georgian architecture, our apartment building fitted in perfectly and was a stone's throw from the world renowned Clifton College, with its spectacular cricket grounds. With the open spaces of the downs and the green parks on the edge of which, you are spoilt with beautiful views over the Avon Gorge and the famous Clifton Suspension bridge. It's dozens of shops, boutiques and galleries, together with an abundance of cafes, restaurants, pubs and wine bars provided a certain ambiance about the place that made it more than special. We even have a Zoo on our doorstep. I knew that we were going to be very happy living here.

I had not lost all of my body hair. I had miraculously not lost my ever faithful moustache that I had been sporting from the day I first grew it. I had also not lost all of the hair on top of my head. My weight loss, however, was becoming a serious concern. I now weighed sixty-eight kilos, a loss of over fifteen kilos over a six month period. My skin had discoloured, making me look transparent. I was beginning to become self-conscious and annoyed at my physical appearance, but also knew that I was not powerless in dealing with these body-image issues.

The turning point came one afternoon, getting on a bus with Kim for a trip into town. The bus was packed with commuters, standing room only. I felt a gentle tap on my shoulder and a young lady had got up and kindly offered me her seat, which I gratefully accepted. What troubled me was the look on her face while she spoke to me, a mixture of sympathy and pity. That evening, back home, I took a long look at myself in the mirror and I saw an old, thin, sick man staring back at me. This had to change. I was now days away from my third chemo session. With the pain and nausea at it's lowest, it was a good passage of time to be in. I decided to go on a binge. I visited the supermarket with Kim and filled the trolley with anything I felt that I could stomach: yoghurts, smoothies, all sorts of pastries and a ton of bread pudding. That evening, lying sleepless as per usual, I decided that it was time to have a lengthy 'tete a tete' with my adversary.

"Cancer!" I silently scream, "So you think you can just invade my body, uninvited? Destroy my life and cause so much pain to me and my family? I have news for you. From this moment onwards, you are no longer in charge. I am the one who will start destroying you, little by little. For me to achieve that, I need my strength back. You will not bully me. I have a plan."

My mind tells me to go climb Everest, even though my body, tells me that I should be climbing into bed.

Everest it is then.

The next day, I began gorging myself. Fruits and pastries still tasted like cardboard and bread pudding like sawdust, but eat them I did, constantly reminding myself that I would not be sick. I also doubled up on the vitamin C. It worked and within a couple of days, I could feel a change in my body. My energy levels were up. I entered the Oncology centre for my third cycle, walking along the corridors with my head held high. The first thing I did, as per usual, was weight myself. I used to dread this. On all previous occasions, the unforgiving scale would spit out a printed reading, revealing that I had lost even more weight. Not this time though. I had gained three kilos. I turned to Kim, triumphantly holding up the reading card as if it was an olympic gold medal. To me it was. Something deep down told me that this was the turning point. Game on, cancer, game on.

***

With the usual gentle care of the nurses, the third cycle was completed without a hitch. I had reached halfway in my treatment and on our way out, the nurses wished Kim and I a Merry Christmas and handed me a large parcel full of goodies to go under the tree. Apparently, every year a group of companies in the UK, such as Marks and Spencer, donate huge amounts of gifts to all cancer sufferers. A wonderful gesture.

As per usual, we made our way downtown for a spot of Christmas shopping. On this occasion I visited Burger King and devoured the largest 'supersize' burger they manufacture, with an oversize helping of fries and coke. I enjoy it, knowing full well that a couple of weeks earlier, just looking at the signage of this establishment would have made me feel seriously ill.

I now knew that I had at least five days of bad side-effects ahead of me and then, it would be Christmas. The boys had decided that they wanted to spend this Christmas with just the four of us present. We would all move into Rory's central townhouse on Christmas eve, spend Christmas day there and then go back home on boxing day. We wanted, as a close family, to recapture the magic of Christmas, as we had done together for so many wonderful years. On Christmas eve, we listened to carols, gathered around a beautifully decorated Christmas tree, topped with a shining star. The next morning, we sat around the same tree, taking turns in opening our gifts. We also all realise that the greatest gift we have, was the gift of life and of being together. Many, many hugs were exchanged on that day.

CHAPTER ELEVEN
MESSAGES AND MIRACLES

Metastatic cancer. What does it mean, exactly? Doing my own research, I discover that in the past, it meant you did not have very long to live. As simple as that. Even with today's advanced treatments and clinical trials, recovery is not always possible. The Doctors and Specialists treating me have always been particularly honest about my condition. They've repeatedly told me that although it is not curable, with good treatment a good quality of life is possible.

So if a cure is not the solution, what is then? A miracle?

First and foremost, I had to accept what cancer had done to me. Living with metastatic cancer is challenging, both physically and mentally. I have often had to talk myself out of a feeling of total hopelessness. I needed help with simple daily activities. My body felt exhausted, having to deal with continuous doctor's appointments, tests, hideous side effects and a scarily high intake of medical pills. Fortunately, I have had the constant support of Kim and the boys by my side. This was just as tough for them as it was for me. I knew they were hurting as much as I was, and this made me more feisty and determined.

As a cancer sufferer, a daily dose of inspiration makes a vast difference to your mental state. Positive messages and constant words of encouragement from family and friends are vital. Fortunately, in my case, I am blessed and spoilt in that instance. Everyday, Kim would read to me, wonderful messages of support and love from family and friends. Just knowing that I was in their thoughts and prayers was immensely inspirational and brought me huge comfort during the tough days.

She had set up a 'WhatsApp Broadcast' system and used this to let close family and friends know of my progress. I would also receive weekly calls while going through chemo, from my brothers Christian and Henri, and my sister Marielle. I could hardly speak most times, as my voice had been reduced to a feeble croak, but just the sound of their voices and the love I felt was immense in aiding my struggle. These are only small examples. If I had to thank each person individually, this book would go on for another thousand pages. You know who you are and I know who you are. I will always be grateful and I will never forget. The point that I'm hopefully making to you readers, is that should you have a member of your family, or a friend, fighting cancer, the simplest and best thing that you can do for them is to offer words of love and encouragement. I was blessed in receiving a huge number of messages. Some two liners, others a lot longer. The length did not matter. Each single word counted. Let me share with you just a few of these.

From my sister-in-law Cathy - Durban.

Jacques and I are over the moon with Gilbert's progress. What a fighter. Too much awesomeness, he will never give up. The power of the mind. His life story has been quite extraordinary and adventurous. He has a great disposition that has served him well during this trying time. He is in my nightly prayers and when I take communion on Sundays. Thinking of you always. Love to all.

From my niece Francoise - Toronto

What a tough road. Hopefully all behind you soon and better days ahead. Thank you for letting me know the latest positive results. What an amazing message to wake up to, I am overwhelmed and in tears. Only way to go is forward. Sending so much love to you both, and Kim you are an angel. Gil could not have gone through all that without your wonderful care and love. Celebrate each day. Love you both.

From my sister Josee - Durban

I have been very happy to read the latest health bulletin. I hope the worst is over and I'm very happy that he is keeping a positive attitude. Well done my boy, remember I am always near you. I pray for you each time I think of you, and at the 5.30 mass everyday.
Lots of love.

From my nephew's wife Pat - Durban

Such good news that he is putting on some weight. The doctors over in the UK seem to have everything under control. We are all praying for you and keep on believing in miracles - they happen everyday. Stay positive and keep the faith, and everything will work out well. We are thinking of him constantly and praying. The power of prayer. He is a real fighter and must keep up his good, positive spirit. Waiting for good news, lots of love to you all.

From my niece Ariane - Durban

Hi Kimmie, I think we've all held our breath collectively for the past few months in the hopes that all this treatment and pain would yield some good news. What we did not count on was that the news would be great!! I know that you've been on a white knuckle ride since Dioul was diagnosed, but now your prayers are being answered. I hope you're allowing yourself a silly dance of joy, some warm tears and a glass or two of Cinzano. I wish I could fly out and have a drink with you guys, but I'll toast your's and Dioul's continued hard fought battle when I get home. Sending you both such enormous love, with big, fat tears rolling down my face. All my love, always!!!

From my cousin and good friend Patrice - Hillcrest

Hey Gilbert, so good to hear some positive news. You, Kim and the boys are constantly in our prayers, thoughts and in our conversations. Man, we miss you guys so much. We miss your enlightening, interesting and entertaining stories. We miss your cooking and wonderful sense of humour. We miss the special dinners and the couple of beers. We miss our chats about sport, and listening to the wealth of knowledge you had on soccer, particularly on the players, and most of all on your club Chelsea. We miss those fascinating stories, shared from your rich experiences in the life that you enjoyed in Wales, the USA and other places....I miss those times I could pop in to see you at Springfield Park and catch up on some news... well to say that Ingi and I miss you and Kim is a huge understatement. We love you guys, you are that unique couple in a million, and to call you, not just 'cousins', but also 'friends' is such a privilege. We are delighted that you are back with your boys, and getting the best treatment in the world, and I know that with the combination of Faith in our wonderful Lord, and your steadfast positive attitude, you will overcome and be 100% again. Lots of love to you all.

From my niece Mylene - Durban

Ah Kimmie, please give my Doo-Doos a big hug from me. It's very heart sore to know that someone you love so much is suffering like that, and there is not a damn thing I can do about it!! Except send words of encouragement. I cannot believe how much your lives have changed. Please know that I'm always thinking of you guys, what a terrible thing he is going through!! Phew, our health is so precious and we just take it for granted. I fly to London on Wednesday, and I hope my Doo-Doos will be okay to see me. Love you both so much, and I am very lucky to be so close to you both.

From my sister in law Monica - Springs

Read a quote in my diary today and thought of Gilbert: 'Celebrate the little things in life, appreciate tomorrow, never condemn yourself to a life without cause to celebrate and be thankful for what you have.' It takes something like he has been through to realise all of that. We will pray extra hard for him. Big hugs and lots of love.

These messages go on and on and every one of them uniquely special. A humbling one is when my sister in law Inge, age 85, writes to me, telling me of the 436 dialysis treatments she has endured over the past four years,

"Enough about me" she says " How are you, Gilbert, you are strong and you've never given up, so you will get well".

Add to this the non-stop signs of pure goodness from people who I hardly know. One of Ryan's friend for instance, tells him out of the blue that although he does not go to church, walking past one the other day, he went in, lit a candle and prayed for me. Another beautiful gesture is shared with me by Marielle, telling me that one of my eldest cousins, Hensy, who I've never spent much time with and spoken to for years, meets up with a friend of hers every afternoon and they both pray for me.

A lady, also in her eighties, from South Africa, who I worked with forty years ago, heard about my illness and wrote to Kim.

" I hear that my favourite person in this world is not doing too well Kim" she writes "He was my strength when I lost my husband, almost a lifetime ago now. Life is not fair, but he will get better. Prayer is wonderful"

At your lowest point, spontaneous texts and emails that informs you that you were in someone's thought can be incredibly moving and uplifting, especially tender messages from children. My young niece Amy writes to me, telling me that she had to do a project on one of the most important event of her life, and she chose to do one about my struggle with cancer.

Tammy, mother of my little nephews Lincoln and Joel, tells me that on a tedious car trip, she suggested a few 'car games' to her young sons to keep them occupied. They thought about it for a while, and said to their Mom :-

" Why don't we all pray for uncle Gilly "

And they did.

In just about every message sent to me, two words always emerge: 'prayers' and 'miracles'.

A miracle? From my understanding, this is an event not explicable by natural or scientific laws and normally attributed to a Saint or Religious Leader. Survival of an illness, diagnosed as terminal, is seen as a miracle. What, therefore, are my chances of being cured by a miracle? Not much, I hear many people who know me well shout out, in jest, I hope. As a Catholic, my Church believes that miracles happen either directly by the work of God, or through prayers to a specific Saint. Before a person can be asserted as a Saint, they must be confirmed as having performed two miracles posthumously.

With total honesty, I do not consider myself as being a 'good' Catholic. I do not attend Mass regularly. I swear, sometimes too much. I am known to say perfectly nasty things about people and do it in a very entertaining way. I am often critical and not very patient. I was also reminded recently that as a youngster, I was a terribly poor loser. Flipping over scrabble boards if I was not winning - I kid you not. On a more serious note, I unreservedly recognise and accept change, such as homosexuality and Gay rights. Why not? Who are we to judge? I am also a strong believer in the right to early abortions. Everything I have just declared openly makes me a 'not a very good' Catholic and suggests that I commit sins on a daily basis. It will also be wholly silly not to acknowledge that the wisdom of the Catholic Church is far, far greater than my own. Having said this, however, I honestly struggle to come to terms with many of its rules and understanding them. Some rules I embrace, others I politely question.

Let's get back to the Scapular, that I now happily wear. The Christian faith sees it as I do, an object that reminds me to live a clean life. The Catholic Church, by my reading and understanding, sees it as an indulgence. A way to reduce the amount of punishment one has to undergo for having sinned. This is an issue which has bothered me since I was a young boy. I was brought up to believe that any sins committed, no matter how small, had to be confessed and a penitence served. We lived in fear that if we are bad, we will burn in hell. I have never understood that ideology and am pleased to have never applied it to my own children. Do all of the comments made above make me a 'bad' person? I seriously do not think so. I cherish my family, have always worked hard, have always been generous and embraced all human beings. Like everyone else I have imperfections, but being thrown to burn in hell by the Devil for having them? I really don't think so. And yes, I do pray, a lot. I pray my way, by speaking often and directly to my Good Lord.

***

My third chemo session was completed and we had to collect a prescription from the chemist, situated in the lobby of the hospital. As per normal, there was a long queue which Kim joined, while I took a seat alongside the pharmacy. Opposite me, a charitable organisation was having a cake sale. On a long table, a large assortment of delicious cakes were on display. I watched as customers lined up to purchase them whole or by slice.

A young mother and son approached the table and immediately caught my attention. The young boy was visibly a cancer sufferer. He was thin, bald and pale with dark circles around his eyes. Like me, he had most probably just endured a stressful chemo session, but unlike me, he was a young boy with so much to look forward to. His Mother asked him to find somewhere to sit whilst she joined the queue. Armed with a paper plate and an enormous slice of generously iced chocolate cake, he looks around for somewhere to sit. There are plenty of seats available. He looks directly at me and decides to occupy the seat next to mine.

"Wow, that's one good looking cake." I tell him, smacking my lips. "Feeling hungry?"

He looks up at me, stares at the cake now sitting on his lap, then looks up at me again with the nicest smile.

He will do well to eat a tenth of that cake, I think to myself.

"Would you like some?" He gently offers in a low, croaky voice.

"No thank you." I reply, "If you feel too ill to eat it now, take it home, you will enjoy it later."

"Yes, I will." He agrees. "Are you also sick?"

"Yes, same sickness as yours." I answer back. "But I bet you'll get better a lot quicker than me. You are a strong, young man. How old are you?"

"I am ten, turning eleven next month." He answers, still looking down at his untouched slice of cake. "Do you also have a lot of pain?"

"Yes, I do." I tell him, my heart breaking, "but it will soon go away. We need to be strong and brave."

"I know," he replies softly. "That's what everyone tells me."

Looking at him, I feel hopeless and angry. Knowing how harsh chemotherapy can be, it is unimaginable to even think about the damage it was inflicting on such a small body, robbing him the joy of a normal childhood.

His Mother had returned and on seeing her, he hands me his plate so that he could use his arms to gingerly get back to his feet.

"Thank you." He says politely as I hand him back the plate.

"Bye my boy, take good care of yourself." I watch him walk away, holding on to his Mother's hand.

At that very moment I pray to God, my way. I beg Him to please take good care of this young boy. If anyone deserves a miracle, he does.

The word 'Miracle' is used often in our daily conversation, such as:

"It would take a miracle for Liverpool to beat Chelsea."

"Thanks to the miracle of television, we can watch the game live."

"Just witnessed a miracle, Liverpool scored against the mighty Blues."

You get the gist. But real Miracles do happen, everyday in fact. Everyone in their lifetime has either heard of a Miracle, or been a part of one. The wonder of childbirth, to me, is a miracle. A massive oak tree rising from a single acorn and the workings you find in a dissected flower, are both miracles of life. There are two miraculous events that I would like to share with you.

The first is a miracle that happened to a close friend and colleague of my Dad. They both worked at the bank in Port Louis. My Dad, in those days, had three jobs going on simultaneously. He would rise before dawn each day, purchase bread from the local baker and sell the loaves door to door for a tiny profit. He would then work at the bank for the day and in the evenings, he was the projectionist at the local cinema. It was a difficult period in his life and this miraculous event, shared with me on many occasions, had clearly touched him deeply.

A colleague of his was diagnosed with skin cancer, melanoma. It was malignant and had spread, with the tumour disfiguring the back of his neck. It looked so bad that he wore a scarf around his neck permanently and was unable to move his head from side to side. The doctors had told him that it was terminal and he had months to live. Like my Dad, he was a Catholic and knew that his only hope for survival was a miracle. They prayed hard and often. He had a young family who were totally dependent on him. One morning, he told his workmates that he felt exhausted and too ill to carry on working. One of his colleagues suggested that on his way home, he should visit Pere Laval's grotto and pray. He reminded him to take an item of clothing with him, rub it on Pere Laval's casket and wear it.

Pere Laval, was known as the Apostle of Mauritius. A Catholic priest of French descent, he was sent to Mauritius in 1841 as a missionary. He spent the next twenty three years of his life on the Island, serving the poor and the uneducated. He had medical training, which was useful to his ministry and he worked tirelessly to improve the living conditions of thousands of Islanders. Having converted more than 67,000 people to Christianity, he died in 1864 at his parish Sainte Croix. The date of his death became a day of huge significance in Mauritius. It is marked as a public holiday, celebrated annually with a festival and huge processions from all corners of the Island to the site of his tomb. On the 24th April 1979, due to his devotion to God, his willingness to help the poor and with medical confirmation that he had performed many miracles, he was beatified - converted into Sainthood - by Pope John Paul, the second.

That very same afternoon, my Dad's friend, took his colleague's advice and visited Pere Laval's shrine. In those days, it was in the form of a grotto, with stone steps leading down from the one side, and up the other. This allowed long queues of Pilgrims to file past his tomb, which consisted of a plaster made effigy of himself, in a glass display on top of his tomb, which was rubbed smooth by the thousands of miracle seeking worshippers.

It was a quiet afternoon with hardly anyone about. He descended into the dimly lit grotto and knelt at the tomb. While praying, he remembered that he had not, as suggested to him, brought along an item of clothing. As there was nobody else around, he unwrapped the scarf from his neck and rubbed it on the tomb, praying for Pere Laval to cure him as his family would endure terrible hardships if he died. At the end of his prayers, he wrapped the scarf around his neck and made his way out. Halfway up the steps, he heard someone call out his name. He looked back, but the grotto was empty. Once out in the sunlight, it dawned on him that he had just turned his head, something that he had not been able to do for months. He hastily removed the scarf and rubbing the back of his neck, it revealed no trace of the tumour. It had completely disappeared. Sobbing, he rushed home to his wife and they both hurried to the Doctor's surgery. The Doctor was both baffled and elated and confirmed that there was no trace of cancer anywhere on his body. He was cured. The next day, he returned to work without wearing a scarf.

Every single time that my Dad shared this beautiful and extraordinary event with me, we both always had a welling of tears in our eyes. A shared, and gentle cry of joy.

The next miraculous event takes place on the tiny island of Agalega. As stated in a previous chapter, the Island had no medical facilities except for the limited services of a Pharmacist and a Midwife. There was also a lack of medical equipment and supplies. Should whatever supply that was needed run out, it would only get replenished when the next shipment arrived, normally once per month. My sister Josee often speaks about the agony she endured on the Island while giving birth to her second child, Brigitte. Due to complications, forceps had to be used to deliver the baby. The device was not used properly and this resulted in horrendous and life threatening trauma to the child's skull. Josee, a devout Catholic and believer in the power of faith and prayer, gently nursed and nurtured her young daughter back to health. Her prayers had been answered.

Prior to that incident, my brother Eric, at the tender age of eighteen months, passed away on the Island. Cause of death - anemia. Today, anemia is simply cured by antibiotics. Back in those days, on a small Island in the middle of nowhere, such a basic treatment was not available. With the slow and gradual destruction of red blood cells and a poor diet, it becomes fatal. Eric, a beautiful boy, with curly blond hair and large blue eyes, died in my parent's arms. His death and burial on the Island had a profound effect on my Parents, siblings and all of Agalegas inhabitants. The scale and depth of the loss was unbearable, and something they knew that they would never recover from. My poor Mother was so distraught that she swore to never dance again, and she never did.

Accepting the reality of the loss was a painfully slow and gradual process. They went on to have more children and on 6th of May 1950, my Mother gave birth to a gorgeous little girl, with sparkling blue eyes. They named her Marielle. She was a healthy and content child, however my parents started to become concerned when she began to show sign of lethargy. Her skin had turned pale and was ice cold to the touch. The

Pharmacist confirmed their worst fear. She was anemic. He felt this was caused by a lack of iron in her body. Knowing that they could not bear the loss of yet another child on the Island, they began force feeding her an iron packed diet of fish, white rice, beans, eggs, watercress and anything which they could lay their hands on with a high iron content. The days passed and her health kept deteriorating. The whole Island prayed for her recovery.

The feeling of hopelessness and sadness of losing her was unbearable. My parents and older siblings took turns in holding her and keeping her warm. It was early one evening that my Dad, holding her, told my Mom to prepare herself for the worst, as he felt that she would not survive the night.

My Mother, overcome with grief, walked across to the small chapel on the Island where she knelt and prayed. She prayed to her favourite Saint, the Blessed Virgin Mary, Mother of Jesus. In the Catholic faith, she was known to intercede on behalf of those who pray to her. Millions of pilgrims visit her sanctuary at the small market town of Lourdes each year, recognising her role as a Miracle maker. That evening, my Mother prayed in earnest to Her, asking her to please save her young daughter's life and in return, promising that if she survived, she would dress her in her image, wearing the colours of white and blue only, until she turned fifteen. Having said her prayers, my Mother returned to the house, fearing the worst. Walking in, she finds Marielle, sitting up on her Father's lap.

"Something strange is going on here." He tells my Mom. "She has perked up and her body's warmth has returned. Maybe she will recover."

My Mother knew instantly that it was a lot more than that. She was saved. Marielle grew stronger and stronger and is today a wonderful Mother and Grandmother. My Mom kept her promise and dressed her daughter only in white and blue until she reached fifteen. Even the schools she attended had to have a white and blue school uniform.

The fifteenth birthday of a young lady, in Mauritian culture, is a major event. It marks her passage to womanhood and is known as 'La fetes des quinze ans'. My parents organised a big party to celebrate her life and give thanks to Saint Mary. I remember that day very well. It would also be the first day in her life that she could wear any colour she wanted. They had a pretty pink dress made especially for her and gave it to her just before the party. She burst into tears, saying that she would have prefered a white and blue dress. However, to please all, she wore the dress that night and looked radiant. The Belle of the Ball.

Today, if you ever have the good fortune of bumping into my sister Marielle in the street, chances are that she will be wearing white and blue. Of that, I am certain.

CHAPTER TWELVE
TURNING FOR HOME

"Should all acquaintance be forgot and never brought to mind......" The Auld Lang Syne, in all of it's glory, was blaring from the television set as Big Ben struck twelve. Kim and I sat cuddled in our small flat, watching the spectacular illuminations of the fireworks display. Earlier, we had danced alone, cheek to cheek, to the commanding voice of Celine Dion, promising us that her heart would go on, and on, and on. For the two of us, this New Year's eve was one which brought more than a handful of mixed feelings. On the one hand, it was time to wave goodbye to a wholly rotten year and on the other hand, welcome in the year ahead and face whatever it had in store for us.

***

It was the first day of January 2017. My next chemo session, the penultimate one, was due in a couple of days. As per usual, a week or so before chemo, it was a good period. My appetite had returned and I kept eating well, putting on the kilos. I still moved about gingerly and stiffly, but was now getting used to mundane things like constant nosebleeds, a swollen face, aching teeth and sleeplessness - and I call this my good period. The fourth cycle, with the usual great care of the nursing staff, was completed without a hitch. We celebrated with our now customary walk into town and I indulged myself by wolfing down an over sized burger and fries.

Chantal had flown into the UK on Christmas day to spend time with her little niece and Sister in London. Her plan was to spend the New Year with Scott in Edinburgh. They would then drive down and visit me on my birthday. It would be an emotional day, as she would be meeting up with her brothers after a period of twenty-five years. The last time she saw them, they were aged eight and five. The time had now come to celebrate our reunion as a family, look to the future and make new memories. We had booked a table at a restaurant close to our apartment to celebrate both my birthday and the reunion. I knew that it would coincide with the time that my side effects were at their worst, but I would make sure to increase my pain killing doses that day. A significant and special day in my life. The first time I would be together with all of my children after many, many years.

Chantal and Scott arrived at our apartment just after noon, followed by Rory and Elinor a short while later. I watched as Rory and her hugged for a very long time. The same show of affection was repeated when Ryan arrived a little while later. Both Kim and I watched them, feeling emotional and enormously happy. Sadly, I could not turn back the clocks, or even attempt to fill the lost years, but what was important was that we were all together again. That evening, at the restaurant, we all began catching up with the past in a positive way and many stories were shared. The next morning, after having breakfast with us, Chantal and Scott made their way back North to Scotland. I wondered how she felt, having met her brothers again after such a long time. I think it's best shown by the emails which she sent me after arriving back in Cape Town.

Dear Dad,

I was so glad to have been able to spend some time with you and get to meet my brothers. Ryan and Rory are exceptional men, and I like them a great deal. It was good to see you with them and how much love there is.

You and Kim have gone through a long journey. I hope that there will soon be rest and calm. It is a tough fight and you have stood your ground. I am sure that I speak for everyone

who loves you, when I say that we are grateful for you and
your strength in going through this. It takes great courage.

Seeing you and Kim together, highlighted how much her
love for you is such a gift. You two love each other very much,
and I'm sure that is what keeps you going on the darkest days.
I wish there was more I could do from here, please let me know
if there ever is.

Much love and hugs,
Chantal

There is so much distance between Chantal and us geographically. But who knows, the Good Lord works in mysterious ways. Maybe soon, we will all be a lot closer.

***

The next couple of weeks passed with some sort of normality. My body was now tolerating the side effects and I kept on gaining weight. It was now time for my fifth cycle, and as horse racing terms go, I was turning for home. A couple more obstacles and the finish line lay ahead of me. The session, as now per usual, went well. The only difference this time was that I felt the severe side effects kick in almost immediately. It was odd, as I usually had the luxury of some good days before this happened. The good news was that the sooner they came, the sooner they would disappear. On the Friday evening, a mere four days after the session, I began feeling a lot better. So much so that the next morning, I decided to go with Kim to the farmer's market, which took place every Saturday morning, in the Church square at the end of our street.

After nosing around for a short while, purchasing some homemade brioches and pastries, we made our way up the street to the supermarket. As we walked in I felt unsteady on my feet and told Kim I needed fresh air. I walked out and the last thing I remember was leaning against a row of bicycle racks before passing out. It only lasted a minute or so, but when I came around, it felt as though I had been out for an eternity. It was the strangest of feelings. Fortunately, Kim had followed me out of the store and grabbed hold of me as I fainted. A fall would have been disastrous, especially with my brittle bones. Coming to, I felt light headed with a loud ringing in my ears. I was laying on the cold pavement with my back against a pillar. Through blurred vision, I see Kim and a whole lot of strange faces staring down at me.

"Darling, darling, are you okay?" She calls out, panic and anxiety etched on her face.

"Call an ambulance"I hear strange voices.

"Is there a doctor about?" I hear other voices asking.

I pull myself into a sitting position and placing my head between my knees. I take in deep breaths of cold, crisp winter air. I look up and find myself surrounded by an army of onlookers, all anxiously offering to help, holding out bottles of water, juices. I assure them that I just had a bad turn and would soon be okay, no need for an ambulance. I said I felt like having an energy drink. The words had hardly left my mouth, that someone had dashed into the store and bought me a red bull. I gulped it down and immediately felt a lot better. Two ladies from an Estate Agency, situated across the road, virtually carried me back to their offices so that I could sit in the warmth and recuperate while they made Kim a cup of tea. The help, compassion and support from total strangers that morning was extraordinary. The type of gesture which makes humanity great.

Having recovered sufficiently, we slowly and carefully walk back home. I call Don to tell him what just happened and enquire what I should do. In his calm way, he tells me not be be too alarmed about it. He felt it was most probably the combination of having chemo and my blood pressure medication. As I had recovered speedily, I just needed to take it easy and discuss it with the Oncologist on my next visit.

This happened a week later, when I visit Doctor Masson and Nick. On telling them about the fainting, the Oncologist advises me that depending on the result of fresh blood tests, they may decide to stop the chemotherapy and cancel the sixth session. I feel utterly disappointed. My body had already tolerated so much and I did not want to terminate the treatment with just one cycle remaining. Again, I email my feelings to Don and this is his reply:

Hi Gil,

Let's see how you feel by next Tuesday. It seems as though you are mentally tough enough for your last chemo session, but maybe your body is crying enough. I would go for it if your Oncologist gives you the ok. Kill and totally wipe out any little resistant nests of cancer cells boet. Give them absolutely no chance of a foothold in your body.

You are going to have a beautiful Summer.

Love,
Don

A couple of days later, I receive a phone call from Nick Robbins, telling me that the Oncologist has decided that I should go ahead with the final session.

***

Today is 14th February 2017. Saint Valentine's day, but a lot more significant to me, it's my last chemo session. After what felt like a never ending marathon, I was at the finish line. I knew that what I had experienced the past four months was life changing and getting back to some sort of normality would take much time and effort. As it was the last cycle, I walked into the chemo unit armed with chocolates for all of the nurses and staff that took such good care of me. Attached to the offering was a thank you card and it read as follows:

Bristol 14/02/2017

To all the nurses, staff of the chemo unit of the Bristol Royal Infirmary.

Today is the last day of my chemo treatment. I cannot speak highly enough of the care, support and kindness I have received from my first cycle onwards. I could not have been treated any better.
There would be too many names to mention, and their particular way in which they treated me during my visits. Your warmth, smiles and friendliness really eased the passage of my treatment, and brightened an otherwise and very trying time.
The work you do is so important, and you all excel at it in every way possible. You have my unending gratitude.

Thank you.

I watched as the final drops of the chemo entered my body. The last session was over. Rory met us at the hospital and we walked into town to meet Ryan and have a celebratory lunch. You've guessed the venue - wrong. We decided to splash out and I indulge in the biggest burger I could find at TGIF. It was an immensely happy afternoon and I was surrounded by three very precious people who loved, lifted and supported me through this horrendous journey. I could not stop smiling. It was now time to focus on my recovery.

A week later, I attend the x-ray department of the Bristol Oncology Centre for a complete set of tests and x-rays. It would last the whole afternoon. Over that period, I would have to undergo the following: NM nuclear injection; whole body scan; CT thorax abdomen pelvis with contrast test and finally, after a wait of three hours to let the nuclear injection do its work, a complete bone, pelvis and hips scan. I was concerned that it was much too soon after my last cycle to undergo all of these tests, but assumed there was a reason for it.

I arrived at the hospital feeling fatigued, sore and nauseous. I was made to drink a litre of some vile, lukewarm liquid and thirty minutes later, had the injection and first x-rays. I now had a three hour wait and while sitting with Kim in the coffee shop, I started feeling faint and nauseous. I asked her to go ahead and find me a vacant toilet cubicle, as I was about to be sick and could only make my way there very slowly. Fortunately, I got there just in time and was violently ill. I spent a couple of hours in that cubicle, either on the toilet or on my knees being sick. Poor Kim kept knocking on the door to find out how I was. I felt weak, exhausted and had a pounding headache. Leaving the cubicle, I swallowed more Tramadols and gathered enough strength to make my way back to the x-ray department for my final scan.

***

On 28th February 2017, we were back at the Oncology centre, for what I felt would be a significant consultation. All of the tests results were in. On arriving, we were met by Nick and after filling in the Stampede questionnaires, we were shown into Doctor Masson's consulting room. This is what she wrote in her report:

I saw Gilbert today and his wife and with Nick Robbins, Clinical Trials Specialist Nurse.

He has recently completed six cycles of Docetaxel and is currently feeling well. I was pleased to let him know that his CT scan has shown a reduction in the size of his pelvic lymph nodes. His bone scan and CT have shown stable bone metastases which represents a healing response, given that his PSA has fallen to a very low level.

He does have some evidence of venous thrombosis in the right side of his pelvis, although this is not involving any major vessels. He has already commenced low molecular weight Heparin over the weekend. I have recommended that he continues this for a total of three months, but it is unlikely that he will require treatment beyond this as he has well controlled cancer and the risk factor of chemotherapy has now been removed now that this has been completed.

We are due to see him again in six weeks. We will then be planning to follow him approximately every three months.

It was good news. Both Kim and I left the hospital in high spirits that morning. If this battle against cancer was a boxing match, I had certainly taken round one.

As soon as we reached home, we called the boys to tell them what the Oncologist had said. Kim communicated the positive news to family and friends via WhatsApp broadcast and within minutes, happy messages of goodwill began streaming in.

CHAPTER THIRTEEN
THE GIFT OF FAITH

"So, this is what chemotherapy is all about." barked the thirty-something, well built, rugby player sitting in the recliner chair opposite me.

"I really don't know what the fuss is all about." he repeated, while flexing his overworked bicep which was bursting out of a far too tight t-shirt sleeve. "A tiny needle prick, then relaxing for hours on a recliner. This is like being on holiday."

Sitting alongside him, his petite, blonde and pretty wife nodded and laughed at everything he said. It was my last cycle and obviously his first. He looked fit and healthy, and it was obviously clear that a copious amount of instant tan lotion was applied to both his and his wife's bodies the night before. They both looked totally out of place in this ward.

He told the nurses within earshot of his prowess on the rugby field. He was a fearless loose forward that was incredibly unfortunate to have never played at the highest level.

"When I'm given the ball, I remain focussed." He boasted. "I know where that try line is and how to get there. It will not take me long to kick this cancer into touch."

Everytime he made a statement, I expect the nodding and adoring wife to jump up and cheer. Instead she kept her emotions in check, but still gave us a 'that's my man' look.

The man was immensely overbearing and pompous, but at the same time, self-confident and clearly self-assured in his abilities. I respected and admired that. When the nurse stopped at my station to check on my chemo flow, I softly asked her what chemo he was on.

"Same as yours." she whispered back.

"Docetaxel?" I mouth silently back at her.

She nodded, winked and we both smiled, a little too broadly and wickedly.

His session ended before mine. He and his wife made their grand exit which looked more like a lap of honour. Not too long afterwards, my cycle ends and on our way out we hear a loud commotion and alarm bells coming from the emergency room attached to the entrance of the chemo unit. Walking past, we could hear the petite blonde wife, sobbing and telling the nurse in attendance that all was well until they reached the carpark. He had a sudden bad turn and began feeling immense chest pains, and his nose had started bleeding. Peering into the room, I see the poor man. Even the fake tan failed to camouflage his paleness. He sat, bent over, holding a bunch of bloodied tissues to his nose, taking in long deep gasping breaths.

Welcome to our unforgiving world, my good man. Welcome to our dismal world.

***

"Apart from some evidence of venous thrombosis, it's all good news." Doctor Masson tells me.

It was at the end of my consultation with her. I stared at her kind face for a while, and decided to pose the question that had been in the back of my mind for a long while now.

"Doctor, I have often heard the term 'being in remission' used, will that ever apply to me?"

"We do not particularly like to use terms such as these," she says assuredly. "You've responded very well to the treatment and we are pleased with the results."

What an articulate and eloquent side step.

"Thank you," I persist, "but with my type of cancer, surely there is a good chance of it coming back - isn't there?"

"If it does, we will find a way of dealing with it, as we've done now." She says firmly but gently. "We will do a follow up every three months - so go out there and enjoy your life."

Kim and I leave her consulting room that morning, feeling enormously relieved and happy. In the privacy of the elevator, we hug tightly. Having witnessed me push the Oncologist for an answer on the probability of recurrence, she whispers in my ear,

"That nasty cancer is not coming back. Have faith Darling, have faith."

Faith. A word that is so commonly used, but what does it truly mean? I understand that there are two types of faith, the natural and the supernatural.

Natural faith is something we put into action on a daily basis, without even realising it. For example, a farmer plants a bunch of corn seeds believing and having faith that it will produce his yearly crop. On boarding an aeroplane, we put our lives at risk, but do so because of the faith we have in the Pilot's ability.

Supernatural faith, however, extends abundantly above and beyond natural faith. It is a gift that comes directly from God. To assume that I automatically have the gift of faith, just because I was baptised and confirmed in the Catholic church, would be seriously wrong.

I am surrounded by people who have supernatural faith and I have watched them thrive in their relationship with God.

Many of my siblings, cousins and friends have the gift of faith. Being struck down by cancer does not suddenly change me and nor does it allow me admission, or fast track me to this exclusive group. Successful marriages and happy family lives are maintained on the principles of faith, love and respect. A perfect example of such a family, is my cousin Patrice and his gorgeous wife Ingrid. Kim and I have witnessed first hand how the gift of faith has helped them and their beautiful children overcome some extremely difficult challenges. I have always remarked to Kim, that being in their company, and that was fairly often, was being in the company of good. They live a life that has always been very inspirational to us both.

Having said all of this, and like the Farmer and the faith that he has in his crops, I have absolute faith in the wisdom and expertise of the Specialists, Doctors, Nurses and medical team who treat me. This brings me to my relationship with the National Health Service - the NHS. Most Britons, as a pastime, have two favourite topic of conversation. The weather and the NHS. Regarding the weather, it is unanimous, everyone agrees that it's always too warm in Summer and too cold in Winter. However, opinions are more divided when it comes to the NHS. To me, it's simple: the NHS, founded over sixty years ago, is not only a great British Institution, but a brilliant model for the rest of the world. Those who criticise it, and there are many, are in my view ardent supporters of a privatised health care system, and in most probability, can afford extensive and expensive health insurance coverage. Having lived in many different countries, I know, with an enormous amount of certainty, that the NHS is the envy of the whole world.

I am alive today because of the treatment I have received from the NHS and each and every additional day I get to spend with my loved ones, is owed to them.

***

A month had now passed since my last consultation with the Oncologist. The normal side effects from the chemotherapy had mostly worn off, but unfortunately had been replaced by dreadful joint pains and stiffness. The pain, significant at times, began at the hips and spreads to my knees, wrists, upper arms and neck. Most days, I can barely get out of bed, lift my arms, apply shampoo or even get dressed. I am now more dependent than ever on Kim and am ever so grateful to have her by my side. I hurt but I know that I'm not alone. Reading dozens of articles on the discussion board of the Survivor Cancer Network, I am amazed at the amount of post-chemo patients who suffer and complain of these exact side effects. I would need to bear with this pain until my next consultation, with the help of the ever present tramadols.

Speaking to my brother Christian, the vitamins fundi, he suggested that I also take a daily dose of 'Hemp seed oil' tablets, so hemp seed oil it is, and a large container finds it's place next to the vitamin C's. Both get consumed at regular intervals. All that was left to do was sit back and wait for relief - so I wait!

As well as the above, I now begin suffering terribly with my teeth and gums. Due to the evidence of venous thrombosis in my pelvic area, I was prescribed a drug called Clexane, which comes in the form of an injection, that I had to self inject daily in my stomach for a period of ninety days. Altogether, with the zarzio injections, I had self injected myself in the stomach 142 times. My stomach area resembled a bruised pin-cushion.

On visiting the dentist, an amiable, smart and energetic young Irishman by the name of Rob, I was advised that at least two of my back teeth, a wisdom and a molar, had to be extracted immediately due to severe infections. However, being on a course of Clexane injections, the extraction could only be carried out after the treatment, due to the risk of severe haemorrhaging. So more pain, more antibiotics and more painkillers.

A couple of days after the final injection, I had the teeth extracted and presto, more complications. The acute inflammation had caused an abnormal condition called oroantral fistula. The infection had perforated the sinus wall, leaving it exposed. Due to the size of the cavity, the only way to address it was by surgical intervention. Rob the dentist, decided that it first needed time to heal and that it was best to wait until after my upcoming consultation with the Oncologist. So until then, nose blowing and sneezing with a closed mouth was prohibited. A soft diet was also recommended - the journey goes on.

* * *

It is mid-June, and it's Father's day. Ryan and Rory visit, and after handing me beautifully messaged cards, announce that they have rented a holiday villa in the South of France for all of us to spend a week in July. They knew full well that it was my favourite spot on the entire planet.

Initially, I was seriously concerned that I could even endure such a journey with all of my aches and pain. It would also be after my consultation and should the pains persist, I felt that I had strong enough painkillers to keep them in check. I told them both it was a superb idea and I was very excited. The rented villa was perfectly located, perched on a hill, just above the charming town of St Paul de Vence, a mere twenty minutes drive from Nice airport. It had all of the required amenities: a swimming pool, a petanque court and sweeping views all the way down to the Mediterranean. The ideal spot.

A week to go before my first 'follow-up' consultation with the Oncologist. The pains persist, and I am a tad nervous on this occasion, going down to the local surgery to have my blood tested and my new PSA levels, post-chemo, revealed. The next day, I am back at the Bristol Infirmary for a CT scan.

It's the fourth of July, and in less than a week, we fly out to the South of France. We are met, as per usual, by Nick from Stampede, and after a chat and the filling in of forms, we make our way to the consulting room. We are greeted by Dr Rebecca

Huckett, Specialist Oncologist, and she makes us feel at ease instantly.

"In terms of your cancer, your PSA is very well suppressed at less than 0.1, which is great news," she says gently. "The most recent CT scan reveals that your lymph node response continues to be maintained and there is no evidence of any new disease. There is also no evidence of any continued thrombosis on your CT scan, so you can now stop the Clexane injections."

Alleluia, all great news, but why am I still feeling so sore? I tell her of the significant pain and stiffness which I'm still experiencing, especially in my arms, shoulders and neck area.

"It is unlikely that these symptoms are cancer related," she goes on. "I just wonder whether you have an element of rheumatoid arthritis, which was masked by the steroids which you were taking during the chemotherapy. I will write to your GP and suggest that it may be useful to have some blood tests done, looking for inflammation."

Doctor Huckett is spot on with her observations. A week after returning from our holiday, the freshly taken blood tests reveal that I now have a condition called Polymyalgia Rheumatica, which causes severe inflammation to large muscles, typically around the shoulders and upper arms area. The only treatment for it? Steroids. It begins with a fairly high dosage and I will need treatment for several years. The relief is quite dramatic and within days, I am virtually pain free. I feel like a different person. The only downside is that this revelation took place after our return from the Cote D'Azur.

CHAPTER FOURTEEN
LOOKING AHEAD

I sit, feeling happy and comfortable on my well cushioned bench under the cypress tree. It is our last day in Provence and what an immensely charming and relaxed week it has been for Kim, the boys, their girlfriends and I. Every morning, the four of them go out exploring neighbouring medieval villages, while Kim and I remain at the villa, relaxing by the pool and enjoying the blissfully peaceful surroundings. They would return at midday, loaded with fresh baguettes, local cheese and salamis for lunch. The rest of the afternoon would be spent in the pool, followed by games of basketball and finally, a family tournament of petanque before sunset.

We enjoyed late candlelit dinners, served outside, under a sky full of stars, and we remained at the long table well into the balmy nights, sharing happy stories. My back, neck and joints still hurt but it is manageable with the help of tramadols, and a good dose of mental toughness.

On Bastille day, we drive into Vence, a beautiful town, littered with ancient cobbled streets and surrounded by ramparts of tall stone walls. After enjoying a sumptuous meal in a quaint little restaurant, we join the locals on the square and celebrate their 'Independence day', with song, dance and fireworks.

That last afternoon, I sit alone under the shade of the tree. I feel very content and relaxed, in a state of slumber even. Through my headphones, the ever present Cat Stevens has been reminding me what a 'wild world' we live in and 'where should the children play'. Before that, Lara Fabian kept screaming 'Je t'aime' and 'Je suis malade' at me, repeatedly. Suddenly, I hear a loud voice coming from the house that jolts me out of my reverie.

"Pastis, Papi!"

Looking up, I see Ryan and Rory, on the patio, both holding up a large bottle of Pastis, as though it were a trophy.

"Get ready Papi, Pastis time!"

A couple of weeks before our Provence break, Rory had introduced me to a couple of classic french films, which we watched together. They were 'Jean de Florette' and its sequel 'Manon Des Sources'. Based on the acclaimed novels by Marcel Pagnol, it was French cinema at it's best and told the story of the lives of a family and a beautiful shepherdess, set in a rural French village in Provence. What really intrigued Rory, were the numerous scenes of villagers continuously drinking Pastis and playing petanque in the village square. A daily ritual almost.

"You have not had an alcoholic drink for over a year Dad," Rory had promised. "The moment we get to France, we are going to enjoy that Pastis together."

Within minutes, the scene was set. A table and three chairs were placed on the petanque court. Glasses, ice, a jug of water and the trophy pastis bottle are brought out on a tray. Rory, having educated himself on the internet on how to properly serve the aperitif, does the honours. First a good dash of pastis, followed by water and only then the ice. Presto, the pastis turns cloudy, almost yellowy white. We clink our glasses and drink. Our reaction is instantaneous and identical. The moment the liqueur and it's distinct black licorice and potent anise flavour catches the back of our throat, we all simultaneously spit out the offending liquid onto the petanque court.

"Tastes like blooming cough mixture!" Ryan screams, gulping down water from the jug.

"Wow, that tasted awful." says Rory, dashing into the house and coming back with three bottles of ice cold lager.

"Well done, I've waited long enough for a cold beer." I applaud. With that we crack open the bottles, more clinks and shared 'santes' and after a whole long year, I savour the gold nectar again. Once a lager lout, always a lager lout.

The French often use the phrase, 'Je suis dans le pastis', meaning that you're in deep trouble.

They've got that right.

***

Soon after getting back from Provence, I'm diagnosed with Polymyalgia Rheumatica and back on steroids I go. It works well and I start to feel a whole lot better. I can now put on a t-shirt without any help and shampoo my own hair. I feel liberated. The only issue is the lack of sleep, but after more than a year of constant pain, that's a great problem to have.

I can now also go ahead and have the minor surgical procedure to sort out the oroantral fistula. As per normal, there is a complication, and the minor procedure lasts an hour and a half. The cavity, being larger than expected, had to be implanted with pig's membrane. It doubles the cost of the procedure. Expensive bacon, but it works, and I am on the mend.

***

In 1969, man walked on the moon. More than forty-five years later, cancer remains the largest cause of death worldwide. One out of four of the world's population will be affected by this heinous disease, which begs the question, why after a four decade war against the disease causing millions of deaths annually, has a cure for cancer proved harder to tackle than the moon landings? Many strongly argue that there are conspiracies to suppress cancer cures. As a sufferer, I totally disagree. These conspiracy theories are false and downright offensive to patients and to the thousands of Scientists, Doctors and Nurses that fight this monster. And why am I so sure of that? Well it's very obvious and simple. Doctors and their family members also die from cancer, every single day in fact. Would an Oncologist let her Child die, or die herself, just to keep a secret cure hidden? We all know the answer to that.

Enough is enough. Together, we can overthrow cancer. The best way of doing that is by supporting and raising money through fundraising schemes. By doing so, we will be helping our scientists and get closer to finding a cure. Just this week, under Ryan's leadership, both he and Rory and three of their friends formed a team and took on the gruelling challenge of completing a 'Tough Mudder' obstacle course. They did it for my chosen charity, being Cancer Research UK, and raised a substantial amount for the cause, well above the target they set themselves. They were awarded special recognition for being in the top five percent of all fund raised, for the month of August in the UK. All of that money goes towards funding cancer-crushing science. Well done to them, I am one immensely proud dad.

I also believe that I have written more than enough about cancer now. Too much respect for a disease that has brought so much suffering to my family and I. It took our Mother from us, as well as my brother in law, Francis. But at the same time, many in our family have survived. My father in law Thomas, my sister Josee, my sister in law Danielle and my good friend Lance. All of them waging a courageous fight and winning. Champions.

Since becoming a sufferer, I have read hundreds of inspirational stories and quotes, but the one that has stayed with me is the one liner sent to me by Marielle - 'Cancer is a word, not a sentence'.

Cancer will not have the final say in this book - hope will.

It is hard to keep track of all of the decisions which I have taken in my lifetime. When making life changing decisions, both risks and rewards need to be taken into consideration. Some I regret, some I am happy with and some decisions were just plain scary to make, but what would be even scarier is if I had lacked the courage to make them.

One such decision, was the one that I made five years ago, selling up everything we had worked so hard for at the worst possible time. I now have no doubt that these dreadful cancer cells had already and unknowingly begun invading my body at that stage. The rewards that this decision brought me were miraculous. I went back and lived on my Island again, lived in South Africa for a period of time and spent loving and happy moments with my brothers and sisters and I was reunited with my beautiful daughter.

I have made my life count by living every moment of it. I have never wanted or needed to accumulate financial wealth, or climb silly corporate ladders, or acquire fancy titles. Instead, my wealth has been the time spent with my loved ones and my fortune lies in the magical life that I have lived, by building one adventure after another, and another.

It is too easy and comfortable to become a creature of habit. Shock yourself, go out there and try something different. Opportunities happen around us daily, grab one. I have, many times.

I now revel in the little things and everyday I watch as dozens of tiny miracles happen around me. A beautiful scenery, fragrance from a flower, a stranger's kind smile, the taste of a ripe mango, the flight of a dragonfly, a bear hug, the break of dawn and even the sound of rain. I have come to realise that these little things, are actually the big things in life.

As I type the final words of this book, I feel content. Better than I've felt for well over a year.

I feel truly blessed. Blessed with the continuous support and love from my wife, my children, my family and my friends. And, as always, close to me, is my medallion.

ACKNOWLEDGEMENTS

Had it not been for the gentle push and prod from my niece Mylene, and sister in law Catherine, this book would have probably never been written.

Who would want to read a book about cancer?

As I began my personal journey and struggle against this awful disease, I felt that by telling my story in an uncomplicated and honest way, it may hopefully help and encourage fellow sufferers.

It began with a paragraph, which became a page, and suddenly the words began to flow freely. Simple and unpretentious, hand written words falling from my mind onto a blank sheet of paper. Pages became chapters, and suddenly I had written the final sentence. There was something very soothing about the whole process. It evoked special memories from my childhood and past, and my wish is that, one day, my great grandchildren will enjoy reading it.

My heartfelt thanks goes to all the Oncologists, Urologists, Doctors and Nurses from Southmead Hospital - Urological institute. The Bristol Haematology and Oncology Centre. The Bristol Royal Infirmary. Wells road Surgery. Pembroke road Surgery. To Nick Robbins from STAMPEDE clinical trials and Cancer Research UK.

A substantial donation from royalties obtained from the sales of this book will go to Cancer Research UK.

I dedicate this book to all fellow cancer sufferers and all those who love and support them. Also to all the victims, and all those who go on loving them.

My endless gratitude as well to both my sons - Ryan, for his foreword and to Rory, for the beautiful designs of the front and back covers. To Lauren Chassebi, for your willingness and kindness in editing the book for me.

To my precious wife, children, family and friends.
Thank you all, thank you so much.

September 2017